And They Called Me Bigfoot

AND THEY CALLED ME
BIGFOOT

The Memoir of
Robert Norwood Clemens

ROBERT CLEMENS

OBOL HOUSE
PUBLISHING COMPANY

An imprint of Huntsville Independent Press

2112 Morningside Drive NW, Huntsville, AL, 35810

Obol House can bring authors to your live event. For more information or to book an event, contact Obol House Publishing Company at +1 (256) 678-0411 or visit our website at: www.ObolHouse.com

Cover design by Chris Treccani - 3 Dog Creative
Interior design by Chris Treccani - 3 Dog Creative

The text for this book was set in Adobe Garamond Pro.

Manufactured in the United States of America
First Obol House paperback edition February 2026

12345678910

The Library of Congress has cataloged the hardcover edition as follows:

Names: Robert Clemens, author.

Title: And They Called Me Bigfoot

LCCN (2024950415)
Identifiers: ISBN 9798992732184 (pbk)
ISBN 9798994369906 (ebook)
ISBN 9798992732191 (hcv)

CONTENTS

ACKNOWLEDGEMENTS

There's no doubt that I worked hard to earn the accolades that I have received over my lifetime, but a person doesn't live the kind of life that can fill the pages of a book without needing to thank a few people along the way.

First of all I would like to thank my parents. The doctor called me a big un' when I came into this world, and the fact that my mother was strong enough to give an unmedicated birth to me in our little dogtrot house back in 1933 says a lot about her. She fed me well, making sure I grew up to be healthy and capable of anything life threw my way. She and Dad both cared a tremendous amount about my education and gave me the drive I needed to become an academic success, despite growing up in a poor rural area. My dad was a hard worker and he expected everyone around him to work just as hard. I didn't always appreciate that as a youngster, but he gave me the type of work ethic it takes to become a success in this world. I am also appreciative that Dad didn't tie me to the farm, though in those days it would have been easy for him to do so. There were times when I'm sure he needed my help in the field, but he saw to it that I never had to miss a game.

I am forever appreciative to the academic institutions that allowed me to earn a great education and master my skills on the football field. To the House of Happiness, Scottsboro Elementary School, Scottsboro High School, the University of Georgia and Golden Gate University, I am eternally grateful for all of the opportunities to learn that were afforded to me within your walls and for the chance to make my mark on the history of your football teams.

To the Green Bay Packers, thank you for recruiting me and letting me get a taste of life as an NFL football player.

Many thanks to the loyal fans who named me "Bigfoot" all those years ago and to those who followed my career as my nickname got shortened to "Foots." I will always be flattered that you saw something in me worth cheering for.

The United States Air Force played a huge role in the story of my life, and I will always feel honored to have been able to serve this great country under its leadership. Without that experience, I would not be the man I am today.

I am eternally grateful to the late John Bates, who presented me with a business opportunity that shaped my second career.

Many thanks to Danielle Kirkland, who made sure that every word in this book was just right. Her careful attention to the writing and grammar played a great role in bringing my story to the page, and I am grateful for her part in making this publication possible.

I would like to extend my sincere thanks to my wife Annette. Thank you for standing by me and for all the wonderful years we have shared together. Thank you for encouraging me to put my memories on paper so that my progeny might always remember the adventures I had around the world and be inspired themselves to get a good education, work hard and build the life of their dreams.

IN THE YEARS BEFORE I WAS BORN

When the Great Depression hit, there were just two radios and one telephone in Sauty Bottom. Times may have gotten a little leaner there when the market crashed, but true poverty had already encroached upon the small, rural corner of the world where I grew up much earlier. An Episcopal missionary had already deemed Sauty Bottom one of the poorest places in Alabama as far back as 1923.

Most families relied on sharecropping and tenant farming to barely make ends meet. However, my grandfather, Thomas Samuel Clemens, owned his own farm, which spanned 160 acres. There were four barns—two for horses and two for mules, plus a few cattle. Each horse had its own stall, and now, ninety years later, I still have one of the old troughs. There was also a pen for pigs.

Maybe it was just luck. Perhaps it was his entrepreneurial smarts. But the hardest of times seemed to escape Grandpa Clemens. The sole telephone line? That was his. He also owned one of the old radios. He even managed, in the middle of the Depression, to buy the first car Sauty Bottom had ever seen. Unfortunately, the state of the roads, which were muddier than a pig wallow and lousy with potholes, didn't make the ride much more comfortable than traveling with his mule-drawn wagon.

You might think it was his inclination for backbreaking work that kept his five children — three boys and two girls—clothed and fed a little bit better than some of his neighbors who were so poor that the day the Great Depression hit was no blacker than any other Thursday. And maybe it was his hard work at first. But Grandpa Clemens, or Uncle Tom

My grandparents, Thomas Samuel and Annie Black Clemens, standing in front of the first car in Sauty Bottom.

A portrait of my parents, Jim and Sue Lee, taken in 1928.

as everyone called him, learned an all-important trick somewhere along the way. He figured out how to hand the burden of toiling labor to others while he supervised.

He handed a portion of that labor to my dad, who, by the way, owned the second radio in Sauty Bottom — a nine-tube True Tone Radio that he had bought from Sears Roebuck.

Dad was born in 1908. His given name was James Norwood Clemens, but everybody called him Jim. He was second to the oldest born, and as soon as he was old enough, he began sharecropping part of the family farm.

He was a workaholic, ambitious like his own father, even as a teenager.

When Dad was 16 years old, Grandpa Clemens, along with some other locals and the county government, came together to improve Woods Cove Road, a significant part of their route to and from town. Working on the road paid $4 for a ten-hour day. It was hard work for a teenage boy, but Dad helped grade the road with a pair of mules and a plow. He wasn't going to miss out on the job or the money.

My parents met when they were 20. Dad was visiting a neighbor, and my mom, Sue Lee Lowe, was staying there too.

Mom had lived with her mother and her grandmother right across the railroad tracks in Scottsboro, and she worked at a hosiery mill. They never talked about it, but I think Dad wanted to give her a better life. So he asked her to marry him in 1928. Somebody loaned them a Model T, and they crossed state lines to Jasper, Tennessee, where they got married at the courthouse.

Their first year of marriage was plentiful. When the Alabama State Bridge Corporation began construction of the B.B. Comer Bridge in 1929, they relocated to Scottsboro so Dad could assist in pouring concrete for the pier. They both made a good living that year, with him earning three or four dollars a day and Mom making three dollars and a quarter at the mill. Working overtime, they managed to bring in $350 in one month. They might as well have been rich for the times.

After living in the city for a year, they returned to the family farm in Sauty Bottom, where they lived with my Grandma and Grandpa Clemens while my dad built our family's first home — a spacious three-room house with a dog run and a front porch.

That year, my parents had their first child — my only sibling, Juanita B. Clemens. She was born in the chill of November and soon caught a cold. They put her down for a nap, but when they went to check on her a little while later, she had passed away. She lived to be only a few weeks old and died on December 9. They couldn't believe they had lost their little girl. She was buried in Finley Cemetery in Scottsboro.

1933: THE YEAR I WAS BORN

My dad continued to farm his portion of my grandfather's land throughout the Great Depression. The corn grew high, and the cotton was at least fair to middling. While the nation's economy hit rock bottom in March 1933, the Clemens family in Sauty Bottom, Alabama, was doing relatively well. They were clean. They had clothes on their backs. And there was always plenty of food to eat.

Franklin Roosevelt became president that year, and his New Deal brought about change to the Tennessee Valley. The US Army Corps of Engineers had already begun searching for a location in Guntersville to dam the Tennessee River. When the Tennessee Valley Authority was formed in 1933, the need for a dam was finally deemed necessary.

Building the dam would make the river easier to navigate for trade, protect farmers from losing their crops due to flooding, and, perhaps most exciting of all, generate electricity.

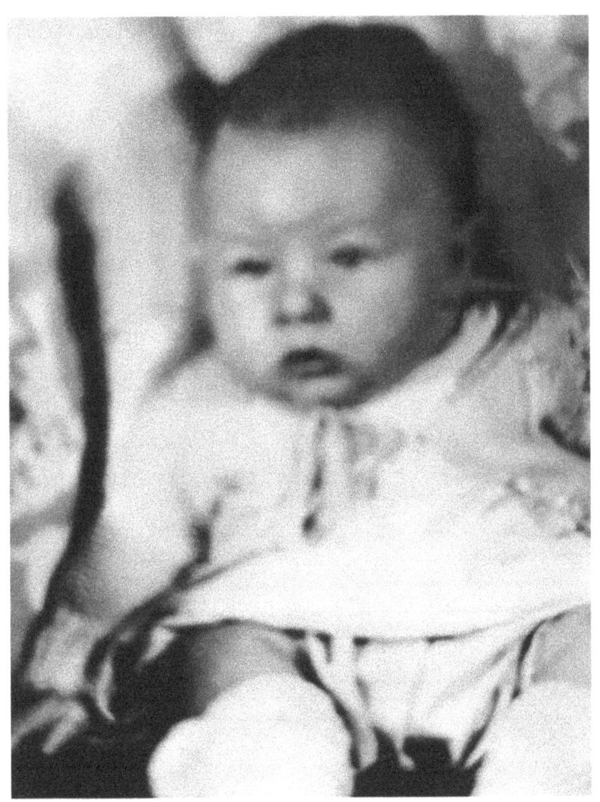

A portrait of me as a baby.

Me safely behind the walls of the makeshift playpen my
mother constructed out of chicken wire.

BUT WITH PROGRESS COMES CHANGE.

To complete the Guntersville Dam project, the government purchased 110,145 acres of land, including part of my grandfather's farm. Everything from the land that was to be flooded had to be cleared. Construction of the dam displaced more than 1,200 families. Homes were moved. Cemeteries were relocated, and trees were cut for timber and firewood.

My dad got in on the tree clearing. He worked for the TVA, making a dollar a day, sawing trees. Of course, after he paid a quarter a day to stay at a Langston boarding house during the week, he only profited seventy-five cents a day.

Before long, he got entrepreneurial himself and bought two mules and a wagon. With the help of his new team, my dad hauled logs from the farmland, which would soon become the bottom of North Sauty Lake, to the sawmill at Guffey Hollow. His pay increased to $2.25 a day.

By now, my mother was expecting her second child. Me.

When the time came for me to make my way into the world, my dad ran down to his parents' house to use what was still the only telephone around. He asked the operator to get Dr. Rayford Hodges on the line so he could let him know a child was on the way. Dr. Hodges arrived in the middle of the night to help my mother along in her labor.

Around 5:00 a.m. on August 3, I was born. There were no scales to certify my weight, but Dr. Hodges declared that I was a "big 'un." That must have been true because my mother had no other children. That was the first time anyone ever called me big, but it wouldn't be the last.

I was a healthy baby, and my mother kept me close by. To ensure my safety, the front porch was enclosed with chicken wire. I suppose you could call it a prehistoric sort of playpen. My mom made my diapers and clothing herself, with a sewing machine she inherited from her mother. They were constructed from flour and fertilizer sacks, fashioned like jumpers that a little girl would wear today. They got the job done, though.

EARLY CHILDHOOD YEARS

I was told I started walking when I was eight months old. Naturally, my memory does not stretch that far back, so I cannot confirm that. One of the first things I can remember about my life is what I had for breakfast. My mother used to make me oatmeal every morning. Sometimes, there would be the addition of homegrown eggs fried up in an iron skillet or ham and fatback cut from a hog my parents killed, smoked, and processed in our backyard. But there was always oatmeal.

Most of my time during those early days was spent on my mother's side, while Dad was away cutting timber or working the farm.

She was a strong and hard-working woman, though she always did what my dad asked her to do. She picked cotton, slopped the hogs with table scraps, grew a garden, and tended the chickens. On wash day, she would heat water in the black wash pot outside and spend hours scrubbing our clothes by hand. I helped her with her chores, and when I got old enough, still in the days before a grassy lawn, it was up to me to sweep the dirt yard.

With the help of a mixed-breed dog named Fido, I gained a little bit of independence from the chicken-wired porch and my mother's hip in just a few years. I wasn't allowed to go anywhere without Fido by my side. Mom would call Fido home, and I'd have to follow. "When the dog comes, you come," Mom would say.

Every morning, a little while after I finished my oatmeal, Fido and I would walk a quarter of a mile down the little dirt road to my grandparents' house, where my grandmother, Nancy Ellen Black Clemens, was waiting with my morning snack— a biscuit and jelly, sometimes ham.

Me and my dog Fido.

A portrait of my dad and I.

Me with one of my dogs and a new red wagon.

There was little chance of us getting hit by a car, for the only modes of transportation around, besides my Grandpa Clemens' car, were mules or horse-drawn wagons. Still, my mother kept an eye on me until I reached the safety of Grandma Clemens' yard.

When the sun set and the day's work was done, we all slept in the same room at night. There was only one fireplace in the house, and our parlor doubled as a bedroom, allowing the family to stay warm during cold winter nights. I can still remember the old dog irons that kept our fires going and the kettle that hung above the fire, where Mom would heat water for dishwashing or taking baths.

There was one visitor we always looked forward to seeing each week, and that was the man who drove the rolling store. Trips to a store in town happened few and far between, but the rolling store brought goods each week for us to buy. Mom would often sell him eggs to pay for salt or other necessary staples. I learned early on that if I sold him an egg myself, I could turn enough profit to get a piece of candy or Juicy Fruit bubble gum. I suppose I had entrepreneurial blood running through my veins as well, and trading with the rolling store was the beginning of my training. As soon as I saw his truck coming down the road, I searched under all the hens just hoping to find an egg.

We looked forward to seeing the ice man, too, but he only came every other week. He'd deliver us a fifty-pound block of ice, and it'd be stored in the smokehouse, where it was covered in sawdust to prevent it from melting. Mom used it for making ice cream and cooling down our drinks.

Every fall, my parents worked together to pick the four acres of cotton my dad had planted. When they finished the hard work of picking, it was time to take the crop to be ginned. Dad would start his five-mile journey down Old Sauty Bottom Road to I.E. Airheart's Cotton Gin in Scottsboro as early as 2 a.m., with his wagon loaded down with loose cotton and his mules leading the way. While many farmers made a day out of going to the cotton gin, packing a lunch, and socializing while they waited in the long line for their turn to come, Dad wanted to be first in line so he could get back to the farm and put in a full day's work.

His drive to get as much work done in a day as a man could do worked against him one morning when he was headed back home from having his cotton ginned with about an hour left in the night before the sun came up for morning. He didn't have a lantern on his wagon, and a police officer wrote him a ticket for it. "Hell! There ain't nobody out here, man!" he said he told the officer. It made him so mad that he told the story until the day he died.

When I was around four or five, Dad let me ride with him to the gin. It was cold as we set off on the wagon, so he dug a hole in the cotton and buried me down in it to keep me warm.

At that time, Dad sold around 500 pounds of cotton and brought home $25. It paid the expenses to make it to another year or to pay off what you owed.

In 1937, after he had made his sale, he went to Grant Lewis's grocery store in town and bought some bacon. I was accustomed to our home-grown pork, mostly pieces of old fatback from a hog that my parents had fattened up in the pig pen and smoked out in the backyard smokehouse. It was the first store-bought bacon I had ever tasted and the best meat I'd ever eaten in my young life.

Store-bought items, like the bacon, were rare. But I did get them from time to time. I recall receiving a cowboy belt with two holsters, and later, I was given a guitar. But in 1937, Santa Claus brought me a red wagon with sideboards. For a busy four-year-old, this was a vast improvement over the inferior regular red wagon that Fido and I had pulled with us as we traipsed around the farm. My new sideboards matched the ones of the farm trucks I had seen. I was stepping high as I pretended to haul hay just like my dad. I am told I even tried to make use of my dog as one would a mule, but I do not recall if Fido submitted to the command of a small child and pulled my wagon like a good boy.

Towards the end of that year, Dad bought 80 acres of property that joined Grandpa Clemens' farm. He borrowed the $700 needed to purchase Jacobs Bank. He continued to sharecrop a portion of his dad's land in addition to the 80 acres. Now, many decades later, I live nestled at the foot of the mountains on the first property my dad ever owned himself.

GRADE SCHOOL YEARS

A few days after my sixth birthday, the Guntersville Dam went online. It took seven days for the water to reach the farm. All my life, people have asked me what it was like to watch the water come up, but there's nothing to tell. We just woke up one morning, and there it was. I had been expecting it.

Maybe it was strange for my family to see farmland that had once been rich with cotton and corn suddenly be drowned by the Tennessee River, but Grandpa Clemens was paid a fair price by the TVA for his property.

Furthermore, the prospect of having electricity was something exciting for Sauty Bottom.

A month later, in September, I went to school for the first time. By now, I had graduated out of my flour sack rompers, and I was wearing Tom Cat overalls. I attended first grade at the House of Happiness, a two-room schoolhouse that was a part of the mission of the Episcopal Church of the Diocese of Alabama.

The little school housed grades one through six, and each morning I walked the one and a half miles from my house to the House of Happiness.

At that time, there were two first-grade classes, first low and first high. Most children back then had no formal training in reading before they began school, having been raised mainly by parents who were uneducated themselves and who almost certainly prioritized farm work over books. Nearly all of them had to repeat the first grade. On my first day of school, there were kids as old as 12 in my class.

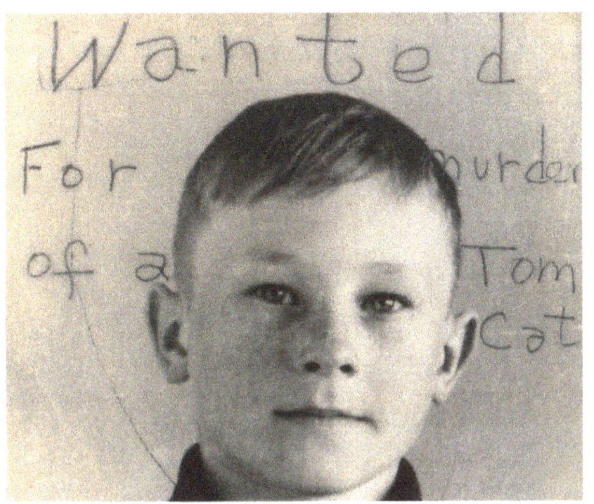

A convicted watermelon thief and accused tom cat murderer.

Me sporting my best overalls before heading to school.

I guess I had a leg up on them. My mother, who had only a ninth-grade education, began teaching me well before my first day of school. Education was also important to Dad, who had a brother and a sister in college. He even became a member of the House of Happiness school board.

To put it bluntly, I may have been the youngest and brightest child in the school. At any rate, I was a hell of a lot smarter than they were. And of course, they didn't have anything, and we had a little bit in the way of money. It didn't take long for the other kids to take offense at our differences, and at an early age, I began to quarrel with some of the older kids.

About that time, my teacher, Miss Brewer, who must have noticed what was going on, began picking me up and driving me to and from school.

While other kids were required to stay home and help out on some days, I went to school every day. When those kids were at school, they didn't pay much attention. I did. I guess I wanted to learn. I was able to finish low first and high first all in one year, irritating my classmates further and leading them to refer to me as the teacher's pet.

Nevertheless, Miss Brewer continued to transport me to and from the House of Happiness until the following year, when the school acquired its bus, which was an old flatbed truck that resembled a chicken coop on the back. The other students and I would ride the bumpy, cherry-red road to school, sitting alongside each other on wooden benches.

In the summertime, I spent my time freely roaming the farm and riding my bicycle, or helping my mom with her chores. I always hated gathering eggs because the hens would peck at my hand when I pulled the eggs out from under them.

My cousin, Scott, lived just down the road. We were the same age, and we spent a lot of time together during those early summers. We would go down to the creek and look for crawdads, and we had a little swimming hole. We'd throw rocks in the water to clear out the snakes before we jumped in. That's where we learned to swim, even though you could only get a couple of strokes out of it.

We got into some hot water once when we got the rascally idea to steal some of our neighbors' watermelons. That didn't pan out too well when old man Coffey caught us. Without hesitation, he reported our misgivings to our parents. Mr. Coffey got his watermelons back, and as you can imagine, the punishment doled out to us boys put a halt to our criminal careers. That was the last time we ever stole a watermelon.

Scott moved away after the second grade with his family, who left for Fairhope, Alabama, to grow potatoes.

That was about the time the House of Happiness school closed down.

Roads had improved to the point where children could be transported more easily to larger schools in the area, and that meant the end of little schoolhouses like the one I started in. My dad was displeased about the decision to close the school. He had even suggested building a new school for students in our area. He was also unhappy that the Jackson County Board of Education intended to send House of Happiness students to Temperance Hill School.

The superintendent of the board was adamant that I enroll at Temperance Hill. Dad wasn't giving in, though. "The hell you are," he said. I guess he didn't think much of Temperance Hill, where classes were comprised of as many as 40 students. He believed I would receive a better education at Scottsboro Elementary School, so that's where he enrolled me.

Due to the rift between my dad and the superintendent, the school bus driver was instructed not to let me ride the school bus. On good days, I rode my bike the five miles from Sauty Bottom to Broad Street in Scottsboro. The road was made of dirt until I turned right on Charlotte Street. It was lucky for me that farm people woke up earlier than city people, and I always seemed to make it to school on time despite the arduous journey.

After a while, my dad found a teacher who had to pass through Scottsboro to get to her school in Larkinsville. That cut my bike ride down to two miles, and I rode the rest of the way with her each morning and afternoon.

The school in Scottsboro was different from the House of Happiness. To start with, I was academically behind the other kids, but I eventually caught up. The kids at House of Happiness hadn't liked me much because my family had a little more money than theirs. But in Scottsboro, there were kids that I'd consider rich, others not so rich. I was bigger and brighter than most of them, and probably the most athletic of them all. My mom kept me clean, and I blended in with the city kids just fine. I didn't think there was any difference between us. We were all in the same boat. I was even confident enough to get one of the wealthiest girls in class to be my girlfriend, but by the third grade, her family sent her to a private school.

1941: A YEAR FULL OF CHANGE.

For the first seven years of my life, our home was lit by Aladdin lamps. Our food was cooled in the deep well where we drew water, or by the chill of the ice we bought every two weeks. This year, however, we finally saw the benefits of the hydroelectricity generated by the Guntersville Dam.

My uncle, who had a degree in electrical engineering from Auburn University, came one day to wire our house and connect us to the grid. During his visit, he installed a light in the kitchen ceiling and an appliance plug for a refrigerator. He did not wire it such that there was a switch on the wall. Instead, you had to pull a string that was attached to the fixture to get power to the lightbulb. I was proud to help him install this new technology in our home as I crawled into the attic with my hammer. He told me where to clang my tool, and I hammered with vigor. It was to his detriment that I missed my mark, and instead of hitting the nail, the hammer squarely pinged his finger. He lived for many decades after this, and at the time of his death, which was sometime in his 80s, that finger still bore the dark blood blister that resulted from my poor hammering skills.

It was that same year that I witnessed a significant shift in the agricultural sector. World War II had been declared a few years earlier in Europe, but by 1941, it began to affect farmers and businesses across America.

A year earlier, the United States started registering men for the draft. When we joined the war after Pearl Harbor was bombed on December 7, 1941, the government amended the Selective Training and Service Act to require all able-bodied men from 18 to 64 to register with the local draft board. My dad avoided being drafted because farmers were considered essential to the war effort at home. Farm workers were also granted military deferments, but a labor shortage persisted, and farmers began relying more heavily on machinery to replace the lost manpower.

That's about the time Grandpa Clemens bought his first tractor. I can still remember the day they unloaded it. It was a bright red Farmall Model H. He had to trade a few mules, and maybe put a little on credit, but the tractor had a two-disc plow that I'm sure alleviated some of the hard work my dad and the sharecroppers had done alongside the mules for years.

A few months after our country entered the war, production of civilian vehicles was halted. No cars were built between 1942 and 1945. When my dad heard that the government was putting a freeze on the sale of consumer vehicles, he rushed to buy his first truck. He knew it would be his last opportunity for the next few years.

He went to Mr. Word's car dealership, where he picked out a 1942 Chevrolet pickup truck. He paid for it by writing a bad check for $700, but early the next morning, he borrowed the $700 from Jacobs Bank to cover the cost.

Until then, our lives had mainly revolved around the farm. I don't remember going anywhere besides school and church before Dad bought his truck. Leaving just wasn't something we did very often. However, the new Chevrolet allowed us to travel and visit relatives and friends when time permitted.

The war might have been changing the world, but school went on normally for the most part. As adults were asked to cut back on gas usage and to plant victory gardens, we children had projects of our own to help with the war efforts. At school, we knitted squares of yarn that would later be sent somewhere and made into blankets for the GIs.

It was about this time that I took a big trip to Tennessee with my Grandpa Clemens. We took to the dirt roads, making our way to my Aunt Nora's house in Columbia. Along the way, we stopped for a rest and a Coca-Cola at a country store, where I saw one of the most unusual sights I have seen in all my ninety years. Besides selling Coca-Colas and gasoline, the little store also served as a bar. Sitting there on a barstool was a man holding his baby. The child was fat and healthy, but when he started to cry, he was not soothed by his bottle of milk. His father poured out the old milk, opened a bottle of beer, and filled the baby bottle to the top. That baby sucked its bottle dry, chugging his way to a brighter mood. The picture of the father and infant son drinking together is one that has remained with me all these years.

When we reached Columbia, Aunt Nora and her husband, my Uncle Hamp— the one whose finger I blackened while installing the light fixture in our house — surprised us by taking us 30 further miles to Nashville, where we got to watch the Grand Ole Opry. Listening to the Opry on Dad's radio on Saturday evenings had been a regular occurrence in my childhood. We were four rows from the stage at the Ryman Auditorium. For a little country boy like me, it was a big deal to look up and see those musicians in the flesh. I talked about it for a long time afterwards.

In 1942, when I was in the fourth grade, the dentist recommended I visit an orthodontist due to a crooked tooth that was perpendicular to my other teeth. The orthodontist was in Chattanooga, and dad drove me to my first appointment, but after that, it would have been difficult for him to drive me to and from all of those Saturday appointments that would fill the next three years. Luckily, my mother's favorite sister lived in Chattanooga, so it was coordinated with her that I would ride the bus to Chattanooga on Saturday mornings. My aunt took me to all of my appointments by streetcar, and afterwards I tagged along as she shopped for silk stockings, which were rationed at the time, and having me along allowed her to purchase two pairs.

I rode a train back home on Sunday. The train made many stops on its route back to Scottsboro from Chattanooga. It was a slow ride back, but my mom and dad were always there waiting for me when I returned. That always made me happy.

As the years went by, my teeth got straighter, and things continued to go well at school. In the sixth grade, my classmate Bill McCutchen and I got in the habit of telling tall tales to our class after lunch. We tried to outdo each other. Sometimes I think back on those days, and I can't believe I did that, but even the teacher liked the stories pretty well.

I began participating in organized sports and playing basketball for a traveling team. The coach would pick us up at school or at home in his Model T. All of us boys would pile in and travel to our games. We usually played teams on Sand Mountain, in Macedonia, Section, Dutton, and Rosalie. Those schools had fourth, fifth, and sixth-grade teams. There were no paved roads back then, and a lot of times, all of us boys had to get out and push the truck through mud holes from Macedonia to Rosalie.

When I got older, I continued to play travel ball rather than play for my school team. The coach would still pick me up, but this time we travelled to places like Chattanooga, Huntsville, and Gadsden to play at YMCAs. With all of the walking and bicycling I'd done in my life to get where I needed to be, it was nice to have someone pick me up and take me to the ballgames. Plus, the coach would take us out for a nice dinner after our games. That's something the school never offered, and it was hard to give that up.

EARLY TEENAGE YEARS

My home was a two-mile bike ride to Sauta Cave — often referred to locally as the "bat cave" or "Saltpeter Cave." It had two entrances, and the lower one was a blowing cave that gave off a cool breeze all year long. The cave is rich with history. It is said to be the place where Sequoia introduced his alphabet to the Cherokee natives, and Confederate soldiers mined inside for saltpeter, which they used to make gunpowder. In the 1960s, along with almost twenty other caves across Jackson County, it was designated as a nuclear fallout shelter.

Sauta Cave is closed off now to help protect the endangered bats that live within it, but during my childhood, it was a happening place.

When I was about thirteen years old, my friend, Bob Matthews, and I went to the cave several times to enjoy the cool air that emanated from within. Inside the cave were electric lights, but we never went past the light because we were too scared of what was back there.

There were different attractions in and around the cave over the years. Once a dance hall was set up inside, later a restaurant, and someone built tiny fishing cabins that people could rent short-term.

But one of the things that drew us young boys to the area, besides that cool breeze back in the days before air conditioning, was curiosity about the bootlegger who lived at the bottom of the mountain just before you got to the cave. People kept the road to his house pretty hot, but not just for the alcoholic beverages. On Sundays, he hosted cockfights. We would ride our bikes over to witness some of the action, because it was something very different from our everyday lives. We'd lurch behind the men who

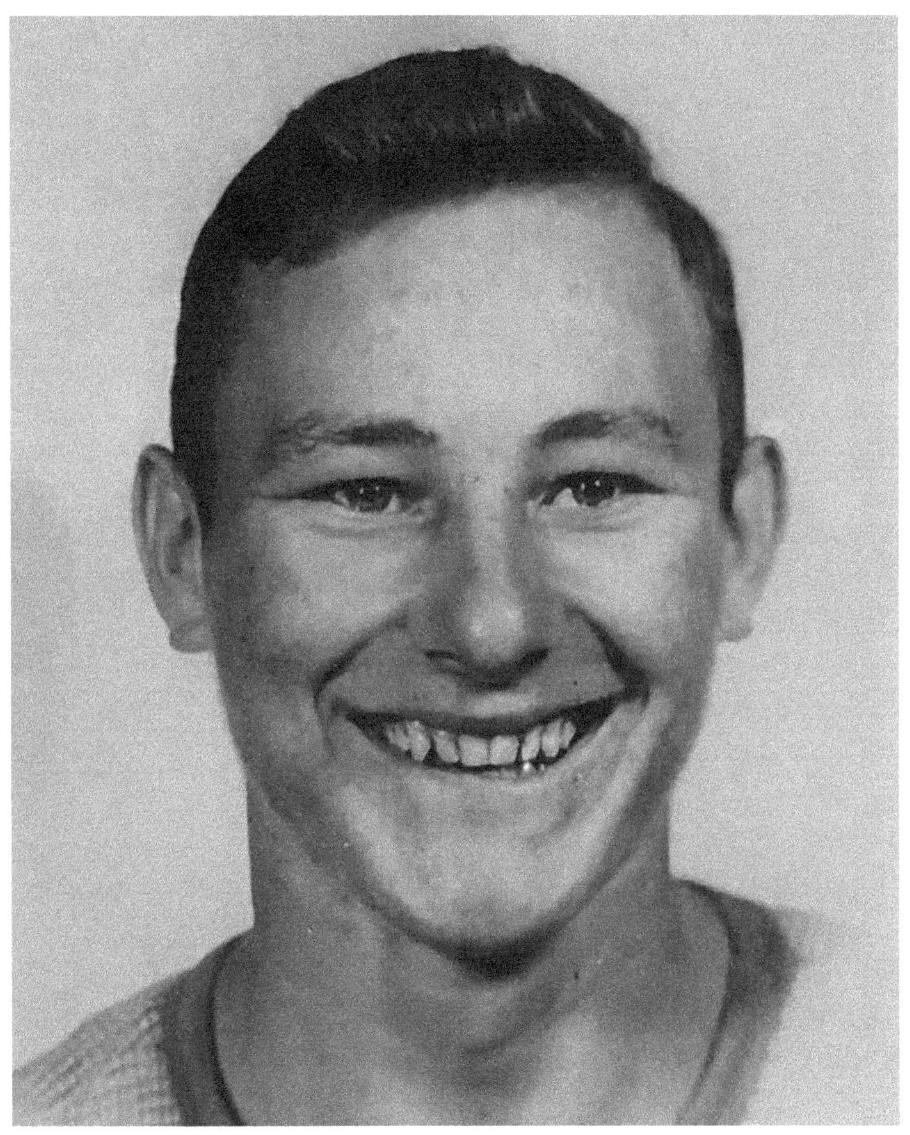

Me as a young teenager.

encircled the cockpit, peaking our heads around them for a better look at the two gamecocks that were inevitably bound to spur each other to death. There was a lot of betting that went on at the fights, and it was big-time money back then. To say the least, this was no place for children. And eventually we'd get run off when someone finally spotted us and yelled, "Get those kids out of here!" Every now and then, someone would grab one of the feathered "losers" and take him home to fry up for dinner the next day. But my dad always told me, "Don't you dare bring one of those old chickens home!" So, I never tried my hand at nabbing a dead rooster.

Junior high started in mid-July, and I was enrolled at Jackson County High School for the seventh grade.

One good thing about being in the seventh grade was that it guaranteed me a ride from my house to school and back on the bus. Unfortunately, I lived in the same area as my bus driver, Mr. Guffey. He picked me up at 6 a.m. each morning, and I didn't get returned home until around 5 p.m. In the wintertime, it was already dark when I got off the bus. That meant I had to do my chores by the light of a lamp in the freezing cold.

The curriculum in junior high was standard for all students. There was only one elective — the glee club. That was not my cup of tea. But when I made it to ninth grade, there were more choices. I chose courses that were college preparatory. Things like Advanced Math, Algebra II, Chemistry, and Physics. Coming off the farm, it felt like everything they were telling me at school was new and interesting. That's why I paid attention. A lot of my friends chose easier routes by taking Ag, but I had enough damn farming at home. Even though I chose more difficult classes, I still made A's and B's.

We completed a quarter of the school year in sweltering classrooms, because come fall, school let out again so everyone could pick cotton.

By the time I was 13, I had been in the cotton fields at picking time for many years. When I was very little, Mom carried me along as she picked, but I had to start helping as soon as I was old enough to carry my own sack. I didn't have a row to myself at first, but I'd just carry my little cotton sack and help my mother. When I got older, I tried to keep up with Dad, who could always pick more than anybody else. His record was around 270, and I tried my best every year to beat him. The closest I ever got was 266 pounds.

Cotton was handpicked until 1951. It was a cash crop, so the work had to be done no matter what. No cotton meant no bills could be paid, and no food could be bought. So, for every year of my high school career, I spent the fall in the cotton fields.

OUR FIRST MOVE

In 1947, my dad borrowed the money from Jacobs Bank to purchase an 800-acre farm a few miles down the road from my grandpa's place. That meant that our family would be moving from our old-fashioned house with the dog run to a new house located at the foot of July Mountain. The new house, which dad hired carpenters to build for us, had two bedrooms, a kitchen, a bathroom, a dining room, and a family room where the big wood heater was located, which was the only heat in the house.

The house had a full basement, but it leaked like a sieve. During most of the year, it was used to store junk we did not need, but in the wintertime, baby piglets sometimes occupied the space. The wind would get so frigid that they would have frozen to death outside, so we took them from the snow at night to get them out of the cold. When it warmed up a little, they'd go back outside to their mama. Sometimes it happened that she would not take them back, and we would have to bottle feed them until we could get them sold.

Despite having pigs in the basement in the winter, the new house was nice. It was the first time we had indoor plumbing and light switches on the walls. It felt almost like we had moved to town and were living like city folk.

By now, I was a full-fledged teenager. My life consisted of school, sports, and any farm chore my dad needed help with, even though he often said, "Hell, I lost you back in 8th grade because you played ball so much."

I felt like driving the tractor, picking cotton and corn, loading logs, or getting cattle and hogs ready for a trip to the sale barn was still a lot of farm work. But it was true that sports began to take a front seat.

In the spring of 1947, the football coach at school allowed me to take spring practice with the varsity football team. That was an eye-opener, because before that, I had only ever played sandlot football.

At age 14, I weighed around 170 pounds, but I was as clumsy as an elephant, and I just barely endured this new way of training. The other players were bigger than I was, and I wasn't used to that. I had always been the biggest. To make matters worse, the boys who had been playing longer had better tackling, blocking, and running techniques. I was too proud to quit, though, and somehow the coach didn't kick me off the team.

That first football season was mainly uneventful. I only played as a tackle in games, but my parents attended my games and supported me. I learned during my first season that being a lineman was no fun. I couldn't see what was going on in the game, and I liked to be where the action was. I wanted to be a running back, so I hung in there. I was determined to improve myself over the summer.

But before I could do that, there was the matter of getting through my first football banquet. The banquet was held in the basement of the lunchroom at school, but for a fourteen-year-old boy, it seemed like a grand affair. I didn't have anything to wear, but my dad solved that problem when he bought me a new shirt and a new pair of pants. I had wanted to double date with my friend Bill McCutchen, but I couldn't find a date, so I just attended the banquet and absorbed the ceremonies, not realizing that in the coming years I would be a featured player. I already had dreams of becoming the captain of the team. I tucked those aspirations away after that first banquet, but I did not forget them.

SOPHOMORE YEAR

Somehow, around this time, I became the first baseman for the Goose Pond baseball team. The team consisted of what were, in my mind, old men. Looking back, I guess they were probably only in their 20s and 30s. It was cow pasture baseball. But on game day, the field was scraped clean. Someone would bring bases and a six-foot backstop, made of chicken wire, which was placed behind home plate.

To tell the truth, it wasn't so much the baseball that I liked as it was the getting out of work. My dad was a six-day-a-week man. He worked that way. But come noon on Saturday, I've got to go play baseball. Losing his farmhand aggravated him, and when things got screwed up, he would blame it on me not being there. But he never objected to my leaving the farm to play sports.

The team never practiced together, but they asked what position I wanted to play. Since my mojo was being where the action was, I chose to play first base because that meant all of the batters that didn't strike out had to come my way.

The home field was two and a half miles from home, and I'd ride my bike to the games. Eventually, I saved enough money to go into town and buy myself a Western Flyer motor bike. It had a small engine that was started by pedaling. It would cruise about 20 miles per hour, and I didn't only ride it to baseball games. I rode my motorbike everywhere, except the town, because my dad wouldn't let me. Eventually, its brakes gave out, and the only way I could stop was to drag my feet on the ground. One day, I was riding on the unpaved roads between the House of Happiness and

The 4-H show steer I won in a calf scramble and trained for competition.

home. I hit a curve and lost control. My Western Flyer got bent to pieces, and that was the end of that form of transportation. It was back to either walking, hitchhiking, or pedaling my old bicycle.

To get to away games, all of the players rode together on the back of a flatbed farm truck. Every Saturday, we all pitched in a dime to help pay for the gas and to buy a new game ball. We played away games at places like Hollywood, Limrock, Grant, and Paint Rock Valley.

Paint Rock Valley was the exception to the title of "cow pasture baseball," because in that town, we played on a real baseball field behind the school. I was the first person to hit a baseball clear over the school.

I became pretty good at baseball, even when I wasn't playing with the old men. I played for my high school's team during my junior year, still as a first baseman. We won the district tournament, but were disqualified because two of our players played for the Scottsboro City Semi-Pro team, and that was against the rules of the athletic association. One of those two players was me. I also played on the American Legion Post team, and in my freshman year of college, I played on my school's team. My baseball career ended there because I could not hit a good curveball. I didn't have time for it anyway. Besides, football was my real passion.

The summer that year was like most others in that it was filled with farm work. By this time, I was my dad's official tractor driver. Since this was the days before hydraulic lifts on the equipment, the plows were raised with the power of springs and human muscle. I may not have realized at the time, but my farm chores were helping add to the brawn I needed to become a football star.

I did take note that I could improve my athletic skills by lifting fertilizer and seed bags, and I may have been the first to discover that manure can come in handy for football training.

Dad used his banker to purchase forty head of cattle, and he pastured them in a small area on the farm. They defecated all around the area where they slept, and I soon decided that would be my practice area for agility training. I'd carry the football under my arm and dart in and around the fresh piles of cow manure. If I stepped on one, I would fall and be covered in the stink and grime of next year's fertilizer. That happened only once, and that accident taught me to always sidestep in the space between the cow patties.

On another part of the farm, my dad had brought in goats to clean off the underbrush. A boy I grew up with and I made our own football field out in that direction where we'd toss the football around and get in some practice between chores. One day, we kicked the football, and a goat jumped out and hovered over it. This was the oldest and the most foul-smelling billy goat on the farm. Since it was nearly impossible to hold our noses and play football at the same time, we found the goat to be both a distraction and a nuisance. From that day on, every time we showed up to play, he would see us coming and jump the fence to see if he could get in on the game. We quickly learned that if we wanted to get any training accomplished, we would have to tie him up and keep ourselves upwind. When we were ready to quit, all we had to do was untie him and kick the ball over in the field where he was supposed to be. He'd chase the ball right back over the fence.

My ingenuity in training paid off. I returned to the football team in 10th grade, ready to run. By now, I was 180 pounds. I was still green, but I was hard. I could run fast, and it was hard to tackle me. I told the coach I wanted to be the ball carrier, and in spring practice, I broke out. The coach noticed my agility and increased speed and decided I would play fullback.

School was still out for cotton picking when we played our first two games that year, so I picked until 3 p.m. on game days, and then my dad would drop me off at Reid's Drugstore until it was time to walk the three blocks to school and get dressed for the game.

We won those games, and excitement over the 1948 football season began to draw the largest crowds ever recorded for Jackson County High School.

One day, my principal, Mr. Couch, called me into his office and asked me how I got home after practice. I told him I rode the train to Larkins-ville and walked the other four and a half miles home. He asked me how much it cost me to ride, and I told him it was fourteen cents. Maybe he didn't realize my dad owned one of the biggest farms in the county, and he thought I was just a poor country boy, or maybe it was because he knew I was going to be the star football player, but he offered to reimburse me for my train fare. I liked the idea, but told him that for twenty-five cents I could pay somebody to drive me home, and I wouldn't have to walk that extra four and a half miles. After about a month, I decided to keep the quarter and hitchhike half the way home.

That year marked the beginning of something. I didn't know it yet, but the next eight years of my life would be spent as a football dynasty. I'd go places and accomplish things that not many other people from small-town Alabama could lay claim to.

I had become the best running back in our district. I was the fastest and once again the biggest.

Another football banquet was held at the end of the season. Dad bought me a double-breasted suit from the Red Hot store in Scottsboro. By that time, I wore a size 14 shoe, but all I owned were tennis shoes. So Dad had a company in Chattanooga make me a pair of dress shoes. They looked like the kind of shoes an old man would wear to church, but it was either them or my tennis shoes, so I decided to go ahead and wear them.

The only issue with the banquet was choosing who to take as my date. I had dated a cheerleader from school a few times after games, but I also still had a relationship with one of the farm girls from the country. After thinking it over, I picked the city girl, Betty Faye. That didn't go over well with the girl from the farm, but in reality, she played second fiddle to the cheerleader, who was also a beauty queen. Such a crowded love life was quite the balancing act for a 15-year-old boy.

Bill McCutchen and I were elected co-captains of the 1949 team and were recognized at the banquet. Whoever decorated for the banquet created cardboard football caricatures representing Bill and me. They were anchored to the speaker's tables, and one was adorned with my number, 54. According to the newspaper's report of my replica, "It was generally noticed that the feet were enormous."

I guess the size of my feet gained as much recognition as the quickness of my tackle. My new name was "Bigfoot."

By the end of my sophomore season, I was being scouted by the University of Alabama. They invited me to come down to Tuscaloosa and attend my first college football game. I looked forward to the excitement. But as it turned out, my ticket was for the student section. Everyone was given a red or black sign, and we had to listen to the announcer and hold up whatever side he told us to throughout the whole ordeal. I thought, "Hell, I came to see a football game. I didn't come to do damn cards." But that's the kind of ticket they gave me. I hated it, and to tell the truth, it kind of soured me on Alabama.

When I wasn't playing or practicing football, or doing farm chores, I was training that year's 4-H project— a young Hereford steer. The 4-H club was something a lot of us country kids participated in back then, and we took it pretty seriously. I am still proud to remember the time I was named the 4-H Club's 1948 Citizen of the Year.

I received my steer in the fall, but I'd won him a year earlier in a calf scramble at the 4-H rodeo in Birmingham. There were five young bull calves up for grabs, and ten boys were selected to catch one. It had rained for three days leading up to the rodeo, so the grounds were muddy. They released the calves, and I quickly tackled one, but to win him, I had to put a halter over his head and get him to the finish line. I wrestled the halter on him and headed for the finish line, but the wet muck caused the halter to slip off, and the calf got away. I was able to grab him by the tail, but I still had to get that halter back on. I knew if I let him go, one of the other boys would win my calf. I quickly tugged hard on his tail and jumped towards his head. I finally got that halter back on and made it across the finish line, with his tail in one hand and his halter in the other.

I was covered in about everything you can imagine, but at least I won the steer. The 4-H director took me back to the hotel, so I could get cleaned up, and the elevator operator asked me what had happened to me. I told her how I'd wrestled a calf in the mud to win him. "Looks like the calf won," she said.

When I received the calf, I had to keep him groomed and train him to obey commands. Most of this work had to be done when I got home in the evening after school or after football practice, and it was usually dark by that time. I worked with lantern light, and I taught the steer to wear his halter and stand handsomely. I also had to keep track of how much feed he was given so that at the end of the project, I could tell whether I made a profit or not. I might not have known it at the time, but the steer was good training for my future business endeavors. I showed him at the county fair and won a blue ribbon. Whether he was really that good or not, I will never know, because no one else brought a steer to show and I won first place by default.

When school ended that year, it was time to take the steer back to Birmingham for one last show. We didn't win a prize at this showing, and after it was over, it was time to sell him to a packing house. That was a solemn moment to take his halter off, put a rope around his neck, and walk away from an eight-month endeavor …like walking away from your mother dying. Tough, Tough, Tough. Even after all the years that have gone by, it still tears me up to think about it. But it was part of the project. Though I missed my steer, I did make a small profit, and I had learned a valuable business lesson. From that point forward, I knew that if I was investing in something, I had to keep track of it and figure out if it was worthwhile.

JUNIOR YEAR

The summer of 1949 started the same as any that had come before it in some ways. I worked on the farm, and I played sports. In other ways, it was a summer of transformation.

The world itself had continued to evolve, and by this time, we had our own telephone. Ma Belle didn't run a line all the way to our house, and my dad had to pick up where the phone company left off. He constructed the last two miles of the line so we could have our own telephone. It reminded me of the Waltons, because there were 22 other households on our party line. Any of the 21 besides us could have picked up the receiver and nosed in on our conversations, and of course, they did. I told a girl I was dating that she better not say anything out of line because there was no telling who might be listening. There was no such thing as a private conversation.

During the summer revival, I accepted the Lord and joined our Baptist Church. I was baptized in the Guntersville Lake near my dad's old farm.

I continued to play on the old man baseball team, and I had improved so that I always batted cleanup. My dad still begrudged the half day of work that was lost when I ran off to the games on Saturdays, but he always let me go. By this time, my agility training for football was over. I was no longer a clumsy boy, but a full-fledged star athlete. There was no need for me to dodge in and out of cow pies that summer.

Since I didn't have to train so hard, I had a little extra time to make use of my new driver's license. When I wanted to take a girl to a dance at the House of Happiness, I had to clean out Dad's pickup truck, which usually

The plow dad made me hook up to our mules to keep the middle of our crop rows clean.

smelled like manure at the end of the day. A little of Mom's bleach and well water deodorized it enough to make the smell tolerable. What little of the odor that lingered did not seem to bother my dates. My girlfriends became more numerous, and so did my problems. But that's the way it goes at 16.

Things took a turn that summer when I was out practicing football by the goat pasture and began feeling a pain in my right side. The doctor diagnosed it as appendicitis and determined that my appendix needed to be removed. I was admitted to Campbell's Clinic in Chattanooga, and the surgery was performed. I stayed in the hospital for three long days. I preferred to get out of farm work by heading to the football field or to cow pasture baseball, but this hiccup got me a vacation. After three weeks of rest, I was able to return to life as usual.

One of my summer jobs that year was to move a 40-ton train car load of iron ore remnants from a railroad car parked at Larkinsville back to the farm. We called it slag. Dad used it for a soil conditioner since it was cheaper than fertilizer.

We didn't have a farm truck; therefore, I had to drive his tractor and trailer and haul three tons at a time. The bags weighed a hundred pounds each and were wrapped in heavy paper so that the slag granules would not leak out. It was a two-week job to remove and stack the bags in our large shed. The heavy lifting was probably good for my muscles, but I didn't think about that at the time. All I could think was it was a hell of a miserable way to spend the summer.

In addition to that drudgery, I was tasked that summer with taking the mules into the city to have them shoed. Tractors had taken on a lot of the mules' workload, but my dad was a stickler for clean crops. He still made me take our mules, Emma and Kate, out to the fields where new crops had been planted to have them get rid of the grass in the middle of the rows.

When it came time for me to take them to the blacksmith, I hitched them to the iron-wheeled wagon and drove them to his shop, where they would have their hooves trimmed and get new iron shoes. It was a seven-mile ride each way, and half of that time was on a US Highway. It took three hours to get there, three hours to get back, and I had to sit on a bucket the whole way. Luckily, I had a nickel so I could at least get a Coca-Cola while I waited.

When I finished whatever work my dad had laid out for me every day, I would run five miles, from my house to the lake and back.

For some reason, that summer my dad bought me a young horse. As a freethinking 16-year-old, I decided to try my hand at breaking the horse for riding. The horse was something to conquer. I'd read about the endeavor in a book, and figured I knew all I needed to know to get the job done. After some wrangling, I finally got the bridle and saddle on him. I took him to some soft, plowed ground near the barn for two reasons. One, so it wouldn't hurt so much if he bucked me off, and two, because soft ground gave him less leverage to throw me.

Someone else held the horse with a rope while I rode. When I got on the horse, he bucked, but it wasn't enough to throw me off. It took getting on and off him three times to make him understand it was okay to have me on his back. It might have been a harebrained idea, since I had no experience training horses, but I figured it was 190 pounds versus 500. The dirt worked in my favor.

I'd ridden mules before and been happy for the ride after a hard day of farm work, even if they did clomp with every step. My horse, though, glided. About once a week, I would take a ride on the majestic creature. Only once did he buck me off. I never knew if he got spooked or stung by a bee, but he came right back to nuzzle me and tell me that he was sorry. I enjoyed riding the horse until I left for college, and Dad sold him. I still have the saddle I used back then.

Come July, it was time for football practice to begin back at school. The coach, who, I guess, saw some talent in me, had obtained for me a new pair of football shoes. They were a size 14 and made of kangaroo skin. The new shoes were half as heavy as my old ones, but I could only wear them during games. There wasn't anyone that we played that I could not outrun to tackle in those shoes.

During my junior year, I became larger, faster, and more agile. Game day continued to fill the bleachers with a cheering crowd. Everybody said they wanted to see Bigfoot. The need to hitchhike back to the farm lessened because college scouts from Alabama, Auburn, Vanderbilt, and several other schools learned my route home and would often pick me up after practice and try to recruit me while they drove me home.

My high school years were winding down, and I was beginning to think about my future. I visited the schools I was interested in, but I didn't get the chance often since I was still my dad's farmhand. During football season, I could only visit schools every other weekend.

In those years, the Iron Bowl was played at Legion Field in Birmingham. I was given a ticket to attend this game by local Auburn alumni. I was also given ten dollars and told to report to the Tutweiler Hotel in Birmingham before the game to pick up my hotel key. After I did that, I bummed a ride from a stranger to the stadium.

When the game ended, I grabbed a bite to eat and found my hotel room, where I went straight to sleep. I must have been extremely tired and suffered a deep sleep, because when I woke up on Sunday morning, I was surprised to find eleven other guys in the room with me. I was lucky to have turned in early and claimed one of the twin beds in the room, because the room was so crowded some of the boys even had to sleep on the bathroom floor.

I couldn't believe the recruiter put us all up in one room. Talk about cheap.

A little while after that, a recruiter for the University of Georgia invited me to see a football game with him in Athens and meet Coach Wally Butts.

After a Friday night football game in Scottsboro, I went to stay with him and his wife at their Guntersville Apartment. His wife — a good-looking woman with red hair —laughed about me having to sleep in their small guest room, which only had a twin bed. But the little bed accommodated me fine, and at 3:30 the next morning, we left Alabama and traveled to the University of Georgia.

Upon Arrival, I met Coach Butts and some of the staff. By then, it was lunchtime, and we were treated to a big roast beef sandwich and a pint of milk. That was the best sandwich I'd ever eaten. We watched the game, met with a couple of the players, and then made our way back to Alabama. I made this trip five more times in my last two years of high school.

In the summer after my junior year, I was invited to visit the University of Alabama. I hitchhiked to Tuscaloosa and then located my hotel. Since it was summer, the campus was all but empty. I had my meals in the cafeteria near the hotel, and they let me eat however much I wanted. The trip was mostly uneventful. I went on a handful of dates with a girl I had met when I was visiting in my freshman year, and the school treated me to a dinner cruise on the Warrior River. Other than that, they didn't do much to try to recruit me. But compared to the 12-hour work days that were waiting for me back on the farm, the trip to Tuscaloosa was ten days of bliss.

SENIOR YEAR

The only thing different from my junior to senior year, as far as football went, was that I began to play defense. I was the biggest and the fastest on the team. I weighed more than 200 pounds, but I could easily outrun the little boys who could move fast as Hell. I also played safety that year.

There was the usual farm work and school work, and I guess I excelled at it all. I was president of my class and voted most popular and most athletic.

When it came time to pick a date for the senior banquet, I stuck with the city cheerleader, Betty Faye, over my country girl. She was a pretty good girl, even if she was a cold old gal. I'd had a lot of dates with her. I may have kissed her once or twice, and she looked pretty on my arm. It wasn't much of a romance, though.

After graduation, a traveling preacher came rolling through town with his tent revival. Betty Faye could play piano by ear, and the preacher needed someone to put music to the hymns. Hell, before we knew it, she married the dude and was on the road to revivals all over the south. I said, That sounds just like her doing something crazy, but we were friends through the years, and I attended the funeral of both her and her evangelist husband.

I spent most of the school year courting different schools and questioning whether the summer after high school would take me to Auburn, Tuscaloosa, or Athens, Georgia. When it came right down to it, I preferred either Auburn or Georgia. One night, the scout from Auburn came

My senior football portrait at Scottsboro High School.

The yearbook photo taken of me after I was voted most athletic and most popular in my senior class.

to my house and was hellbent on signing me. I called the scout from Georgia and told him that if he didn't get over there, I was about to sign with Auburn. He hightailed it there, and around midnight, I made the decision to be a Georgia Bulldog.

When I threw my hat up in the air with the class of 1951, I wasn't sad to see my high school days come to an end. For me, it meant getting out of the cotton fields.

ATHENS, GEORGIA: THE SUMMER OF 1951

A few days after graduation, Bill McCutchen and I hitchhiked to Athens, Georgia, for summer school. We wanted to get acclimated before our first football season started, and I had no intentions of working on the farm all summer.

Bill and I shared dorm room 211 that summer. Our college dwelling was the size of a small jail cell and was furnished with two little beds, a chest of drawers, and a telephone table. Bill would eventually switch schools, but that would be my home for the next four years.

When it came time to register for classes, I signed up for Contemporary Georgia and Psychology. I also had to pick between Army ROTC and US Air Force ROTC. The Army Colonel showed me an M-1 rifle. He told me I would be tasked with keeping my piece clean and operational. When I talked to the Air Force sergeant, he handed me a small stone. "Put that in your left hand," he told me. I asked why. "So you can remember to lead with your left foot when we march," he answered. His explanation made my decision easy. Keeping up with a rock seemed like a lot less of a hassle than cleaning a gun. Air Force, it was. I didn't know it at the time, but that would be one of the biggest decisions I'd ever make in my life.

I will never forget the class Contemporary Georgia, not because of what I learned, but because of how the teacher treated me. I made a 95 on his examination, which I guess he thought was too good a grade. He accused me of cheating and made me retake the test. I retook it with the SOB standing over my shoulder. That time I made a 94, and I guess that satisfied him. I wanted to give him the finger, but I didn't. What was really bad about the whole situation was that he turned out to be one of the athletic advisors. Everywhere the football team went that year, that old gray-haired professor was there. And he'd run over Jesus Christ and his grandma to be first in line for chow when we were on the road. I hated that bastard.

In the middle of the second session of summer school, I found out I had been selected to play in the Alabama North-South All-Star Football game in Tuscaloosa. Without telling any of my teachers, I picked up and hitchhiked to the Alabama campus.

I played for the North team, and after about three or four practices, we had our first game at Denny Stadium. We lost to the South team by about 20 points, but I ended up gaining the most yards for my team, which was quite a feat because there were two All-American players in the same backfield.

A former competitor from Fort Payne wound up on the North roster with me, and we became friends that summer. He attended Vanderbilt University, and we were opponents on the football field for three more years. Many years after college, we reunited when I started a business in Huntsville. He was a prominent attorney and represented me in two lawsuits. He was a good enough lawyer, but full of bull. Always was. We still call each other SOBs.

When I got back to Athens, I found out I should have let the school know I was leaving. I have a few WFs on my transcript because of it.

FRESHMAN YEAR

One hundred and thirty freshmen showed up for the first day of fall football practice. I was issued a leather helmet, and I used my shoes and shoulder pads from high school. After two weeks of practice, I was sixth at fullback. The boys who placed ahead of me had a little more training in the basics of blocking and tackling than I'd gotten in high school. It didn't bother me to be sixth. I knew I'd show them what I could do when the time came.

After another week of training, the freshman loaded a bus and headed for Tuscaloosa, where we would play the University of Alabama's freshman team.

Since I was from Alabama, the coach let me start out as a fullback. On the first play, I ran through the entire Alabama team for 70 yards and scored. I had a hell of a night, but there was not much time to revel. As it turned out, showing them just what I could was a backfiring mistake.

Alabama must have gotten their feelings hurt that I'd been recruited by Georgia, because they called for an NCAA investigation to find out just why I hadn't chosen Tuscaloosa. I didn't see daylight the rest of the year as the coaches removed me from the freshman team and hid me on the taxi team. I spent the rest of the season learning plays off a whiteboard and running the schemes against the varsity starters so they could become familiar with their opponents' plays. It was murder for a freshman, since there were several All-American tackles on the starting lineup. I got my ass kicked every time. It was hell, but it kept the attention off my talents, and the investigation eventually went away.

Good luck to you always
Boots !
William Lotts

I figured out later that Alabama must have wanted me to block for the two All-American half-backs they had recruited that year. But I liked the setup at Georgia, and that's why I chose them.

In the midst of beginning my freshman year of football, the fall semester also began, and I declared myself a General Agriculture major. I'd grown up on a farm, and a life in agriculture was all I'd known. I figured with an education, I could win a few arguments with my dad about the way things ought to be done, but eventually I'd learn that even with a college education in agriculture, Dad was and always would be the boss when it came to farming. In the years to come, I'd be standing in the field with my dad discussing crop placement. "What about putting the corn over there?" I suggested. He turned toward me, squared his hips, and then placed his hands on them. "What the hell do you know?" he'd ask me. I knew then that I was finally done with farming, as I whispered under my breath, "I'm out of here."

My classes over the years included math, physics, English, chemistry, entomology, animal husbandry, poultry, cattle, horticulture, soils, forestry, agricultural engineering, genetics, and Air Force ROTC. I made the Dean's List occasionally, and only every once in a while did my grades suffer because I got distracted by a female in my class. Between my coursework and football training, there wasn't much time for a social life. I had to get my flirting in where I could, and I guess physics class was as good a place as any.

After I registered for winter classes that year, football practice began. I was relieved that I could finally come out from underneath the cover of the taxi team, and "You ain't seen nothing yet" was an understatement for what we endured while vying for a spot on the varsity team.

Half of the 130 freshman players didn't return to practice, either due to failing grades or not being able to hack the grueling training schedule. Winters in Athens were cold and wet, but that did not deter practice. After class ended at 2 p.m., we headed to the field and trained until darkness fell. Then we walked a mile back to our dormitory.

When my freshman year was over, I headed back to Alabama to spend the summer with my parents. As soon as I got there, I discovered that Dad had a plan to get me acclimated back to farm life. First, I had to dig out the manure in the mules' stall and spread it on one of the fields. Then he had me clear out the brush and briars from the fence row next to the TVA woods. It was the middle of June, hot and humid. I felt like I was being punished for going away to school. I sweat so much that I had to drink a gallon of water in the morning and another in the afternoon. I didn't like the work. But I showed him, by God, that I could do it.

In the time between chores, I dated a few different girlfriends and worked on staying conditioned for football season by running, lifting weights, and eating sensibly. My mother, who gave me a little warmer welcome than my dad, cooked me good country food that nourished me all summer long. My only request was that she not use so much lard.

SOPHOMORE YEAR

The summer, full as it was of hard work, passed quickly, and before I knew it, I was hitchhiking back to school. On September 1, 1952, my career as a varsity football player at the University of Georgia officially began. After a year of being hidden away, everything felt like a brand-new experience. I competed for the starting job as fullback. I wanted a lot of playing time with the "big boys." I set my goal at number two fullback. My speed was better than the competition, but I was lacking in blocking on pass plays. I figured by the time he graduated, I'd be number one.

You've heard of two-a-days, but for us it was three-a-days. My day began with a mile-long walk to practice at 5 a.m. When that was done, we walked a mile back for breakfast at eight. At 11 a.m., it was time for the second practice of the day. After class ended at two, we would once again practice until dark. The fundamentals of football were stressed, and evening practice was two and a half hours of pure hell. Lucky for us, it got dark early, and that prevented us from having longer practices. After dinner, which was served on tin trays that had been left over from the Navy in WWII, the team met at the film room and watched black and white films of our upcoming opposition.

Our first opponent that year was Vanderbilt. I survived the pre-season training, and we boarded the train bound for Nashville, where I would play my first official game as a varsity player. The game was held on a Saturday morning, and I was happy to look in the stands and see Mom and Dad there to cheer me on.

A copy of my Georgia card.

The team warmed up together, and then we were divided between offense and defense. I was put on the offense. I started the game on the bench— the worst seat in the stadium. All of a sudden, Coach Dupree called me in to replace the fullback. The quarterback handed me the ball, and I gained four yards. I was explosive. It was as if I was reliving that freshman game in Tuscaloosa — only this time there would be no investigation and I would not be hidden away for the season. The coach had known I could get the yardage and knew I was the best they had. I scored the first touchdown of the game.

The same thing happened in the second half of the game. I only needed one play to score from eight yards out. In the last quarter, my roommate returned a punt for 102 yards down the sideline in front of our bench. I scored again, and we beat Vanderbilt that day by one point.

Since Nashville was so close to home, I rode back to Scottsboro with my parents for a visit after the game was over. Of course, that also gave me time to visit with one of my girlfriends before I had to thumb a ride back to Athens the next day.

Fall quarter was set to start on the Monday after the Vanderbilt game, and a new dorm opened along our route to football practice. In it lived freshman girls, so we began to call our path to and from training the "sweater check" route.

That Monday, I spent most of my time registering for my sophomore classes. Football players were given pens, notebooks, and books. All of my books were new, because no other football player was an Ag major. The Athletic Association also paid for the cost of my dorm, which was $360.

During that first week, I began to get more practice and repetitions, which I hoped meant I would be getting more playing time in the game that Saturday. We were set to play Tulane, an SEC member and a tough opponent in the 1950s. I did end up getting more playing time, but I also ended up getting a broken nose.

When we returned to Athens, I was fitted for a face shield. It couldn't be attached to my leather helmet, so I received a new, state-of-the-art helmet with a shield fastened on the top and fixed to close the chinstrap. I was glad to have it, as it helped reduce the impact of all the forearms that went across my face that season. Unfortunately, when my nose healed, I had to go back to wearing a normal helmet. For the last three games of the year, the hits were back.

My social life that year transformed me into a different person. In my freshman year, I'd dated mostly high school seniors. But in my sophomore year, I, along with two of my teammates, chanced to be invited to dinner at the best-known sorority house on campus.

The theme of the evening might as well have been "Country Come to Town." There I was, an old country boy, sitting in an elegant dining room with fifty good-looking and refined women. There was porcelain china and fancy silverware laid out in front of me, but I didn't know a salad fork from a hay fork. My buddy Charlie was twice as country as I was. And my roommate might have been a Yankee from Rochester, New York, but he ate like a horse — didn't have a lick of table manners.

I made it through the dinner and thanked the hosts, but it had been a wake-up call for me. The embarrassment of not knowing how to act in a sophisticated social situation was worse than the pain of being tackled by the world's largest lineman. From that point forward, I made it a priority to learn dining and social skills so that I would be at ease at future social events.

Being on the football team may have been enough to satisfy the egos of the other boys. Eating with them was like eating with a bunch of damn animals, and most of them had no desire to better themselves. But I knew I wanted to become a polished gentleman. I traded in my country fashion for new white Buck shoes and a sports jacket. I ditched my country brogue and learned to speak proper English.

I'd had a taste of the finer things at the sorority house dinner. I liked it, and I wanted that lifestyle for myself. I began looking for a fraternity to become a part of. Sigma Chi asked me to join, and I went through the mind-bending 24-hour ritual of initiation. I was selected, and am thankful for having become a Sig for life. To tell the truth, I didn't care for being in the fraternity too much. But I knew it was an important learning tool, and I meant to take every advantage of it. I began having my Sunday dinner at the fraternity house and attended visitations at sorority houses on Milledge Avenue in Athens. By the end of my sophomore year, you couldn't tell me from the rest of them. No one would have known I was just a farm boy from a poor town in Alabama.

In addition to becoming somewhat of a sophisticated man about town that year, I had finally secured the number one fullback position on the 1952 team.

When the winter quarter ended, I went back to Scottsboro for the holidays. By the time I got there, the farm work had been finished for the year. My dad gave me a new Browning 12-gauge shotgun for Christmas, and I spent the break hunting ducks and geese that landed in the corn fields on the farm. Of course, I snuck in a couple of dates with two of my hometown girlfriends.

When Christmas break ended, and it was time to head back to Athens, I knew I had a gruesome task ahead of me. I'd lettered at the end of the football season, and initiation was waiting for me before I could officially earn my G for the 1952 season.

Initiation is performed with no supervision, and it gives former lettermen the chance to do to someone else what was done to them. Many of the tasks were too horrifying to mention. If you can believe it, one of the less demeaning demands was that we pick up a marshmallow with our butt after sitting on a chunk of ice for five minutes.

After several more cruel tasks, we were transported twenty miles from campus and dropped in the wilderness at two in the morning. Our challenge was to make it back to school in time to attend the first class of the day. The temperature was in the 40s, and I was wearing nothing but a sweatsuit. In my mind, I said, "You can turn me upside down, but I'm going to live through this. To hell with you."

So the others and I found our way into the nearest town, Watkinsville, and discovered that the post office was unlocked. We crowded around the sole lightbulb and took turns trying to warm our hands. One guy decided he'd had enough and jumped on the back of a semi truck and rode it the five miles back to Athens, but I wasn't interested in that mode of transportation.

When the postmaster finally arrived that morning, he found someone to drive us back to school, and I made it to my first class of the day.

The new lettermen had to be back in the center of town at noon to meet the demands of our initiation. For the last task, someone cracked an egg and dropped it from the window of a second-floor building. I stood down below with my hands tied behind my back and tried to catch the egg in my mouth. After two tries, I caught one and swallowed it. When that was done, I walked to the center of the street where I had to bend over, grab my ankles, and spell Georgia one letter at a time as someone hit me in the butt with a large belt. After that, the initiation was complete. I had earned my letter.

JUNIOR YEAR

ootball practice for the 1953 season began on February 1, and we
learned about a new SEC rule that would change the game for the
rest of my college career. From that point forward, once a player
came out of the game, he couldn't go back in until the next quarter. That
meant all teams had to be functional on both offense and defense.

Before this rule, our coaches could run 10 players in the same position
if you wanted to, but normally, you had four people for each position
on offense and defense. The new rule kept teams from having unlimited
substitutions.

For me, the rule change meant that I would be a running back on
offense and a linebacker on defense, which I hated. In an effort to get
more playing time, I would also be the kickoff kicker because I could kick
the ball further and straighter than the others. I also had to learn to punt
and then pay defense. My longest punt was 79 yards in a game against
Tulane, but I only got credited for 59 yards because I hitched it from the
7-yard line.

The first scrimmage of the season was not good for me. On an offen-
sive play, I ran into the defense and made a start cut. Something popped
in my left knee, and I went down. The injury required an operation, and
it was scheduled with a doctor in Atlanta at the end of the spring quarter.

After the surgery, I went home to Alabama with a cast from my hip to
the top of my ankle and spent a week on the farm for spring break. I went
back to Athens on crutches and made sure to schedule all of my classes as
close to the dorm as possible.

I had to wear the cast for two months, and I began rehab before school was out for the summer. When the quarter ended, I knew I would have to rehabilitate myself over the break. I brought a weight device for strengthening back home with me, and I made a 120-yard straightaway in one of the pastures for wind sprints. Five times a week, I ran the two and a half miles from my house to the lake and back, and I still had to do farm chores for Dad.

I returned to Athens early so I could train by running the steps at the stadium. I was surprised that after all of my summer rehabilitation, I still lacked strength.

I continued to condition myself until practice began on September 1. Since I missed most of spring practice, I had to work hard on the defensive side to learn how to be a linebacker and call the defensive plays, since there were ten different defense formations with stunts on some of them.

The first ten days of training were hell. Like before, we woke at 5 a.m. for a workout, returned to the dorm at 8 a.m. for breakfast, rested until 11 a.m., worked out for an hour, had lunch, and regular practice began at 2:30 p.m. and lasted until dark. Then we'd walk the mile back to our dorms for supper on a tin tray and report to the film room to study our opponents until 9 p.m.

Our first two opponents that year were Tulane and Villanova. Those were our first games with the new substitution rule, and I was still dealing with my injuries. Injured or not, I helped lead the Bulldogs to victory in both matches, with 86 yards against Tulane and 117 against Villanova. I came out of those first two games leading the SEC in rushing. By this time, my fans were calling me "Foots" — short for my high school nickname "Bigfoot"— and I was considered one of Georgia's best.

The new substitution rule proved to be a problem right from the start. One of my best friends, Perkins, was the number four tailback. During the Villanova game, the left half-back position sustained a few injuries, and the number three was injured so badly he had to leave the game. Coach Butts, who was very uptight at games, was frustrated and yelled out, "Who we got?"

There was only one guy left. The assistant coach called out, "Perkins."
"Perkins?" Coach Butt raised his eyebrows and questioned.

Since everyone else was injured, my buddy got some playing time. He eventually lettered that year.

That season was my best one yet. I played well enough to make the all-opponents team for Auburn, Alabama, and Mississippi Southern. For the team itself, the season wasn't so great. The Bulldogs lost eight games and only won three. We'd mourn the losses until Monday, and then hope for better as we spent the next week preparing to face our next opponent. But the rule change, paired with the fact that we didn't have enough players, didn't give us much of a chance. Even though we had an All-American quarterback and end, we just couldn't deliver that year.

During this dismal season, I met the woman who would eventually be my wife and mother to my three children.

Her name was Lillian Remelle Moore, and she was a pretty one. In 1952, she'd been crowned Miss National Peanut Festival in the Dothan pageant. Even though I found her attractive, it was not love at first sight.

Her roommate was dating my roommate, and at first, the relationship was one of convenience. My roommate's lady was the daughter of a doctor and had her own vehicle — a convertible to boot. Lil told her roommate that she had wanted to date me at the beginning of the semester, but I guess I'd had a relationship go south and wasn't in the mood for love.

A date with her got me a free ride in her roommate's car, though, so I figured that made the whole thing worthwhile in the beginning.

Soon enough, I saw past the lure of the convertible, and I began to fall in love with Lil.

When we played the Georgia-Auburn game in Columbus, Georgia, Lil and her roommate drove down and met us for the weekend. After the four of us had dinner together, we all stayed at a local motel. We flipped a coin to see who slept on the box springs or the mattress. Lil and I won, and we took the mattress. The next morning, we noticed the car of the University of Georgia president parked right outside our room. It wouldn't have looked good for members of the football team to be shacking up in a local motel, so we waited for him to depart before we checked out.

Before we headed back to Athens, we cruised by a frat house near the Auburn campus to see a friend of mine from back home. To this day, when we are in a group of people, he always tells the story of ol' Clemens visiting him at school with a beautiful girl in a new convertible. I'd come a long way from the pickup truck on the farm.

The football season ended with a game against Georgia Tech, which we lost.

When the game was over, there was nothing left to do but hit the books and study for fall finals. My hard work paid off when I was named to the 1953 All Southeastern Scholastic team. I went home for Christmas and began thinking about the year ahead.

1954: WHAT A YEAR!

In my senior year, school required a lot of my time because the courses became more difficult than in the years before. I was voted by my teammates to be the alternate captain of the 1954 team. And of course, spring training was as rigorous as ever. We were just like the postal service — Neither snow, nor rain, nor heat, nor gloom of night, stays these football players from the swift completion of their appointed training.

I knew going into spring training that Georgia didn't let seniors play. We were supposed to be comforted by the fact that they gave everyone this treatment, but not getting much playing time still put a damper on my senior season. I was required to do the same training as the freshmen, sophomores, and juniors. Even though I knew there wouldn't be much reward for it, I treated practice just like a game. I tried hard. I still wanted to beat the guy next to me.

I added punting and kicking to my abilities to try and gain more playing time, since I knew if I left in a quarter, I couldn't go back in until the next quarter. My competition was also a punter, and if I wanted to stay on the field, I knew I had to be better than him.

After the spring game, it was a great relief to know that I would never have to endure another spring practice in my life.

When winter quarter was over, at the end of March, Lil and I traveled to Panama City, Florida, to visit her parents. Neither of us had a car, so we rode a train from Athens to Panama City, and the entire trip took over a day.

My college portrait from the University of Georgia.

Me as a Georgia Bulldog.

Lil's parents were great people. They welcomed me with open arms, and I suspected they hoped I would marry her. She had another year of college, and it wasn't easy for them to support the costs of her college requirements.

Perhaps, they got their wish a little sooner than they'd hoped for.

One day, Lil's mother left the house to run to the grocery store, leaving us two twenty-year-olds alone. We took too much advantage of the solitude, and a day later, we rode the train back to Athens in coach, holding hands and feeling very much in love.

A few weeks went by, and then Lil broke the shocking news to me. "I am pregnant," she said. We were just college kids and didn't know what to do. In a panic, she took another pregnancy test, but the results were the same. I wish I could say I had been excited, but the news was a kick in the gut, and I'm certain I felt disappointed.

On April 23, two days after Lil's 21st birthday, we spent the weekend in South Carolina with our roommates. A justice of the peace performed our marriage ceremony.

Needless to say, it wasn't the wedding of our dreams. On Monday morning, we went back to class and continued to reside in our own respective dormitories.

When the quarter ended, we went our separate ways. She went home to tell her parents, and I returned to the farm in Sauty Bottom to break the news to my folks. I didn't break the whole news, just told them I had gotten married. They were very disappointed, even though I assured them I would stay in school, finish my degree, and get my Air Force commission.

I guess I didn't have to tell them the whole truth. My dad filled in the blanks. "I bet you're having a baby," he said.

I spent a few weeks at home and then took a bus to Panama City to spend the rest of the summer with Lil and her family.

Lil's time in Athens was over. When it was time to report back for the start of the quarter, she stayed home. I returned to Athens alone. The coaching staff knew I was married by then, but they told me I could keep my scholarship and continue living in the dormitory.

I had used the beach to develop my stamina over the summer and returned on September 1 in what I thought was the best condition of my career. I pushed myself so hard that I peeked out a week early. By the last week of training, my muscles were overtaxed. I began to lose my stamina and lag behind the others just before the hard training ended.

Somehow, I retained my starting position, but with the unspoken rule about seniors not getting much playing time, my time on the clock became shorter. I still punted and kicked off, but not always.

When I did get to play, it seemed the other team was coming at me hard. In the first game of the season, a Florida State player put a knee in my ribs. After that, I was required to wear a different type of shoulder pads. In the next game, I received a separated shoulder. That required me to wear larger shoulder pads. Luckily, they didn't hinder my performance.

The whole season, I only carried the ball 50 times, five yards per carry. I scarcely played, and couldn't help but feel sour about it. It was no consolation to me that the younger guys needed the experience.

Lil came to see me at the Florida State game and the Auburn game. We spent those evenings together, but that was the extent of our newly-wed life at that time.

The 1954 season for the team was a little better than the last. We won six and lost three.

We should have beaten our rival, Georgia Tech. But we were out-coached by the legendary coach Bobby Dodd. Two plays I remember were a trick play that failed us, and a 52-yard punt that I kicked from our end zone on a cold and rainy day. A few years later, I had the chance to talk to Dodd about the game, and he told me that they had scouted us and knew exactly what we were going to do and practiced against our plays.

Georgia elected not to play in a bowl game that year, but my season was extended because I was chosen to play in the annual North-South Shrine Game. I would spend Christmas in Miami.

As soon as my finals were completed in December, I boarded a flight from Atlanta to Miami.

I was on the South team, and our accommodations were terrible. It was a famous hotel, but it wasn't on the beach, and the only other occupants that week were two old women who were in their forties and not much to look at. Our meals were tailored towards their requests. You can imagine the dissatisfaction among the football players that week.

Lil was due on December 31, and I thought I'd have plenty of time to play the game and get back to her for the birth of our child. But the baby came early. Almost as soon as I was in Miami, I got word that Lil had given birth at the hospital. We had a daughter, and named her Willa Sue— after our mothers. She weighed 7 lb and 4 oz and was 21 inches long. The hospital personnel said she was healthy and everything looked normal.

Lil and I talked it over and decided I would remain in Miami because we figured this might be my chance to be drafted by the pros, since there were so many professional coaches there. Plus, they paid me $100 and gave me a watch and a sports jacket.

My wife and child were in the hospital for two days before they were released and allowed to return home to Lil's parents' house. Communication was short between us, because collect calls from Miami to Georgia were expensive. I didn't let myself worry too much, though. My mother-in-law was meticulous in everything she did, and I knew they were in good hands with her by their side.

Practice went well. I was the number one fullback, and I thought I was going to play a lot of offense that game. I loved offense. What really ticked me off about the whole thing was that another coach and his players arrived about two days before the Christmas night game, and they took over my position. I was then moved to play left side linebacker and never got to play a single down on offense. We played in front of a sold-out crowd and lost. It didn't help our team much that the North team had Johnny "The Golden Arm" Unitas for their quarterback.

When the game was over, I flew back to Atlanta and went home to Alabama from there. I didn't go straight to where Lil was with her parents and Sue, because Mom and Dad had bought me a new Oldsmobile Super 88 and I needed to pick it up.

The next day, I drove down to Blakely, Georgia, where Lil's parents were now living, to see my wife and child. I was anxious to see Sue, but I did not know how I would react. By the time I got to her, she was 10 days old … a beautiful baby, even if she was sort of long and skinny. "What about that?" I thought to myself. And just as I had suspected, my mother-in-law had everything under control.

It was almost time for the winter quarter to begin back in Athens. Lil, Sue, and I loaded up in my new car with Sue's baby bed and a few household items and headed back to school. It was time for us to attempt to live together as a family. We found a three-bedroom apartment on Milledge Avenue— where only a few years ago I had visited a sorority house and stared my journey of refinement.

I moved out of my dorm room, and the athletic department paid me the amount it would have cost to live and eat there. That covered the cost of our apartment.

Everything slowly evolved into a routine of classes and helping Lil survive. Most of her time was spent caring for Sue. She was a good mother, but there were a lot of things she didn't know how to do around the house. Like me, she'd grown up an only child, and her mother had done her laundry and cooking. I guess when you're in love, it doesn't matter if your girl knows how to cook or wash dishes. I knew enough to teach her a few housekeeping skills, and Lil was a fast learner. I guess she had to be.

One thing that benefited us was the fact that I was good friends with the chef back at the dorms. He quite often put aside a few good steaks for Lil and me.

One day, when I went to pick up our steaks, I happened to notice a telegram that had been pinned to the bulletin board in the common room. It had my name on it, and it was from the Green Bay Packers. They wanted to draft me. I immediately went down to the Western Union and replied that I was interested. It was a good thing I went for the steaks that day and happened to look at the bulletin board.

Three weeks later, another telegram came. I had been drafted in the 7th round, and Green Bay wanted to know if I would accept a salary of $7500. I sent them another message telling them that I would.

I wasn't too excited about it. At that time, two years of military service were required for all men.

Playing professional football was just something to fill the gap between the time I graduated from college and the time I had to report to the Air Force. I signed my contract with the Packers on February 17. Art Daley, a longtime sports editor for the Green Bay Press-Gazette, called me a "212-pound speed merchant from Georgia." I guess at that time, I may have been the heaviest half-back Green Bay had ever seen.

I could have graduated from college at the end of that quarter, but after careful consideration, I figured it was more profitable to stay in school. By this time, I was a major and squadron commander in the Air Force ROTC, which was the best of the six other squadrons. The government paid me a dollar a day for being a Senior Air Force participant. That, paired with the hundred dollars that the athletics department gave me since they didn't have to give me room and board, made the decision to stay in school an easy one. Since my course load was low and football was over, I had time to get a part-time construction job in the afternoons. It paid minimum wage, which was $.75 per hour.

My last quarter of college was uneventful. I graduated on June 5, 1955, with a bachelor's degree in Agriculture and a commission as a 2nd Lt. in the United States Air Force. I wore my ROTC uniform, and Mom, Dad, Lil, and Sue came to watch me graduate. It was a nice day.

A SEASON WITH THE GREEN BAY PACKERS

By the time I graduated, I knew that my starting date for the Air Force was March 16, 1956. That gave me roughly a year to play professional football with the Green Bay Packers before my pilot training began.

I moved Lil and Sue back to Blakely so they could be with Lil's family as I got acclimated to life in Wisconsin.

My busy schedule and the stress of raising our first child had taken its toll on our marriage by this time. I was disgusted with the whole damn thing, me and the whole situation. Everything just blows up in your face, and there you are sometimes. Our departure was not a sweet one. I guess Lil said something to tick me off, and I left Georgia and my little family in a cloud of dust.

A few miles down the road, I hit a straight stretch of highway, and I bore down on the gas pedal as hard as I could. By the time my Oldsmobile hit 130 miles per hour, I felt like I was floating. About that time, I snapped to my senses and realized I was nuts. I never wanted to go that fast in a car again.

I went back home to visit my mom and dad for a few days before I made the rest of the drive to Wisconsin. There wasn't much farm work to be done since it was the end of planting season … just a little plowing in the cotton and corn fields. The tension was high between Dad and me. He always got mad at me when I screwed things up, and I sensed that's what he thought I had done with my life. He had a good heart, but I'm sure he was disappointed with the mess I got everything in. My mom was kind about the situation I found myself in— getting a wife and child before I meant to and all.

After a week on the farm, I pointed the Oldsmobile north and made the three-day drive to Stevens Point, Wisconsin. I arrived on July 1 with nothing but my football shoes, and I had no idea what to expect. There were a hundred other guys there just like me, and we were all vying for a spot on the team and the payday that would follow.

Our accommodations were the dorm rooms at a junior college that had been abandoned for the summer. The school was located so far in the boonies that the only way in was by bus or car. I roomed with another player. It felt like I was back in college until I got on the practice field. Then it was more like being back in high school. Not because of the coaches or the other players, but the equipment was all worn out. The helmets were leather. It was shoddy stuff, but we all accepted it and tried our best to beat out the next guy.

At the end of each day, a roster was posted with the names of the players who would get to return the next morning. That was a tough thing for us players to endure, especially when one of our friends was dismissed. I felt like I was riding the fence and never knew which side I was going to fall off on. But I always found my name on the list.

I was the only guy with a good vehicle. The rest of them drove clunkers, if they drove anything at all. I saw my having the only decent car around as an opportunity to cash in on. The rest of the guys made $25 a week for incidentals, but I finagled my way to $50 because I agreed to drive the players who got cut back to the bus station. Hey, you don't get anywhere if you don't ask.

By the end of tryouts, my trunk was filled with remnants of lost dreams … football shoes and special pads from the departed. It had been their last hurrah. Some of them had ridden three or four days on a damn bus just to get there and try out, and it was all for nothing but a ticket home. That's it. That's business. Those guys didn't want the damn stuff anymore. I threw it all away after a while.

We practiced for seven days before players arrived from last year's team, and then the competition got tougher. The guys who played the year before accepted me because of my new Oldsmobile 88. All of them drove pieces of junk just like the rookies, except last year's number one draft choice, who drove a new Buick Riviera. After practice, they'd let me tag along on the beer calls at the local taverns.

The competition might have been tougher, but practice was easier once they arrived. It was a good thing, too. The weather was extraordinarily hot for a Wisconsin summer. Between the heat and the humidity, it must have been a good breeding ground for Polio, because there was an outbreak in Milwaukee that summer. It didn't affect anyone on the team, but we did have to stop drinking after each other.

By the end of July, there were around 50 players left, and it was time for our first pre-season game against the New York Giants. The team loaded up on a DC-4 and flew to Spokane, Washington, where the Giants were holding their training camp.

It was an interesting flight for someone who was going to be a flyboy. The DC-4 was a propeller engine. This was all before the jet age. The trip took forever, I thought, but the scenery was something else. We flew so low and close to the mountains that it looked like I could lean over and spit on them. It was captivating to fly over all of the rivers, the railroad tracks, and the highways. I could see everything.

I played mostly on special teams during the game. I was the wedge buster. One of the most memorable moments for me from that first game was when I almost tackled star player Frank Gifford. I had the chance to tackle him behind the goal line on a kickoff, but I missed him. Somebody else caught him about five yards past. If I'd gotten him, I would have had him for a touchback. But that's the way it goes.

We flew back to Stevens Point on Sunday night. I checked the list, and was happy to see my name still on it. It was about this time that I received a message from the Montreal Alouettes in Canada. They wanted me to be their running back.

I told the Packers' coach, Lisle Blackbourn, about the request and asked him whether he thought I'd make the Packers or not. He told me that I would, so I declined the offer from Canada. It wasn't a hard decision. An old country boy is going to Canada? It just didn't register. Plus, they didn't pay hardly anything.

After that, we took a two-week trip south for a couple of pre-season games. One in Greensboro, North Carolina, and the other in Charleston, West Virginia.

I mainly played special teams again, because we had three running backs. I learned linebacker, strong safety, flanker, and all punting and receiving key positions. I remained the wedge buster.

When the trip was over, we returned to Stevens Point. The final list was up, and I had made the cut. That was good news. I was officially a professional football player, and that meant that after the next game, I could start collecting on my $7500 salary.

I loaded my car with my belongings and as many of my fellow players as could fit. We drove from Stevens Point to Green Bay and were put up in the Green Bay Hotel, which was five stories high but had no elevator. They served a decent dinner, though.

In the middle of September, I received notice from the Air Force that I was now eligible to be sworn in as a second lieutenant. On September 19, 1955, I went into the Air Force Reserve Office in downtown Green Bay and asked if an officer was available to swear me in. There was a lieutenant there who could do the job, and he administered the oath. Little did I know that every two years from this date on, I would receive a pay raise. This was a very important day for me, but later that afternoon, I attended football practice as usual.

The money from the Air Force and the Packers couldn't come soon enough, because I received a letter telling me that my dad was flying Lil and Sue out to be with me.

On the day of their arrival, I met Lil at the airport and with the help of one of my teammates, I found her and Sue a place to stay at a boarding house until I could find something more permanent. Meanwhile, I stayed at the hotel and continued to have my meals there.

That Sunday was our first game. We played the Detroit Lions at City Stadium. During that game, I needed to block a 280-pound defensive end on extra points and field goals. I'd asked around about this guy because I only weighed 200 pounds myself. Since I knew I couldn't block him, I spent the game misdirecting him. We won 20-17.

I don't remember the excitement of winning our first game as much as I remember how happy I was knowing my first check was coming that Tuesday after practice. I was broke, and so were all of the other guys. By the time I got my check, which was written for $632.50, all the banks were closed for the day. Lil and I had four cents to our name and only one bottle of milk for Sue. My wife, with her pageant queen confidence, convinced the manager at a supermarket to cash the check for her. I had to loan a couple of other players a few dollars until they were able to get their checks cashed. It's funny to think now about a couple of professional football players struggling to buy a bottle of milk. Today, NFL water boys probably make more in a month or two than we did for a whole season back then.

The next week, we played the Chicago Bears at Wrigley Field. Another game meant another payday. With debts finally caught up, Lil and I would have money to eat out and go shopping for a few household items that were needed since we found an apartment to rent by the shore of the bay. Lucky for me, it was located next to a tavern, and since I was a Packer, I never had to pay for a beer.

But some bad news was announced at practice on Tuesday. The NFL had adopted a split roster for the season, which meant our roster went from 35 to 33. That meant that two of us could no longer dress up for games. I guess I drew the short straw, because I wound up being one of those two. I was moved to the practice squad, and my pay was cut to $250 a week. I could have gone home, but I thought better of it because the pay was still more than minimum wage, and I didn't have anything else to do before reporting to the Air Force.

Life was still good. I was still a Packer and was still treated like one. But I missed playing in games.

My main purpose for staying was to act as a substitute for a receiver, linebacker, or defensive back if anyone got injured, but as the season rolled on, no one got hurt or replaced except for one safety. The Packers got a player from another team to take his place. I wasn't fast enough. I wouldn't have stood a chance covering a great receiver on a deep pass. So I remained on the practice team until the week of Thanksgiving, when the coach told me and the other practice player that we were no longer needed.

I picked up my last check the next Tuesday, and that was it. Just like that, I was done with the Packers and done with football. Playing professional football had been a good way to ease out of a way of life I'd been living for almost a decade.

MY BRIEF STINT IN PUBLIC EDUCATION

With my football career behind me, Lil, Sue, and I left Green Bay and headed to Alabama for Thanksgiving dinner. After one of Mom's good home-cooked meals, I dropped Lil and Sue off in Blakely once again, and I headed to Atlanta. I needed work for a few months, and my time as a Georgia Bulldog meant they knew me there.

I was walking in the middle of downtown Atlanta when I heard someone holler "Foots!"

I didn't know this man from Adam's house cat, but we chatted for a while, and I told him I was in town looking for a job. As it turned out, he was the athletic director for the city school system in Atlanta. He invited me to his office and offered me a job teaching math and coaching the boys' B team. I didn't know a thing about teaching math, but I could do math, so I took the job.

Later that day, I found my family a furnished apartment located ten minutes from the school and went back to Blakely to tell Lil and Sue the news.

I started my short-lived teaching career on December 1. The days were long since I had to stay after to coach basketball. They were made even longer by the fact that the girls practiced before the boys could have use of the court. It was always dark by the time I arrived home.

The good thing about being a teacher in December was that I got paid for a whole month, but because of the holidays, I only had to work two weeks.

We split most of the holiday vacation time between Lil's parents and mine, but there was also a life-changing doctor's appointment.

Over the past six months, we had noticed that Sue was not progressing like she should. There had been a few instances we thought could have caused the lack of development. She had a clogged tear duct that doctors had to operate on, and little Sue cried and cried from the pain. She also ran a very high temperature with an illness once. Regardless of the cause, the doctor, a specialist at Vanderbilt University, told us that Sue had an intellectual disability and would never reach the mentality of a one-year-old.

He also said it was likely that she would not live past the age of twenty. We were heartbroken for our child. Sue was a lovable baby and quite easy to please. That helped us, but the next couple of years were so sad as we continued to witness her struggle and experienced the fear of not knowing how long she would live. The situation was hard on two young parents who were already having a hard time in their marriage.

Despite this terrible news, come January, I had to report back to school. For the next two months, I was busy nonstop with teaching and coaching. The schedule was hard on us.

Academics were something else. I taught algebra 1 to eighth graders and business math to sophomores. I'd taken two algebra courses in college, but didn't know a damn thing about business math. It wasn't too hard to figure out, though.

The school sent me to the board of education building to be evaluated to teach algebra, since I didn't have any teaching credentials. I think they thought I was going to stay there forever. The man who tested me informed me that I wasn't simple enough to teach eighth graders algebra. I guess he thought I was too intelligent to break it down for the kids. I looked him straight in the eye and told him, "I've been called simple all my life, and now you tell me that?"

He just laughed, and I went back to figuring out how to be an educator.

I knew in my time there that I wanted to really teach the kids something. The eighth graders didn't seem to even know how to measure, so I took two weeks to teach them about weights and measures. I said, "Dammit, if they don't know anything else, they will know this." I thought it was something practical that they could use for the rest of their lives. They learned it too.

My business math class had its ups and downs, I guess. It was as educational to me as it was to the students. I'll never forget the time I told a female student to be quiet, and she threw a book at me.

After school, I was either holding basketball practice or carting around a car full of eighth-grade boys to away games. I had the whole damn team in my Oldsmobile, and the school never even offered to pay me for gas mileage. To make extra money, I had to run the clock for the high school basketball games.

I must have been a decent coach because my team won the 1955-56 championship for Atlanta B teams. It felt good, but wasn't really that big of a deal.

When the season ended, the athletic department wanted me to coach track in the spring. I didn't know anything about track except that there was a 100-yard dash. Luckily, come March, my time working in the public school system was up. I was glad to never step foot in that place again. The teachers were the biggest bunch of bums I've ever met in my life. The teacher's lounge was a filthy place where they smoked and told some of the God awfullest, crudest jokes you ever heard. I'd be embarrassed to even repeat them. And it wasn't only the guys, but the women too. I thought, what a cruddy bunch of people to be around. I wasn't going back to that if I had to go chop cotton.

March 10 was my last day. It was time to report to San Antonio for my Air Force physical and the next chapter of my life.

THE BEGINNING OF MY AIR FORCE CAREER

After my last day teaching, I took Lil and Sue back to Blakely, as was becoming our tradition. Then I headed for Lackland Air Force Base for my orientation.

It was a stressful first week because I knew I couldn't weigh more than 199 pounds to qualify for pilot training. Pilots have to be light and agile. Every damn physical I took during my career, I had to fight like hell to meet the weight requirement. That first time was no different, especially since my football weight had been 210. I didn't eat for three days before that first physical, and thankfully, I weighed in at 198.

Most of the other guys were commissioned officers from ROTC, like me. We all got a month of advanced pay and vouchers to pay for our tailor-made uniforms. The dress uniform was tan and was the best-looking and fitting of all the uniforms I had during my Air Force career.

After 30 days of intense orientation, it was time to choose my first duty station. I was given four choices— Texas, Oklahoma, Georgia, or Florida. I chose Graham Air Base in Marianna, Florida, since it was located closest to Lil's family.

I rented a trailer that would hook up to my Oldsmobile and packed up Lil, Sue, and our three pieces of furniture. We were off to our first assignment.

My Air Force portrait.

GRAHAM AIR BASE. MARIANNA, FLORIDA. 1956

I was always fascinated with airplanes, even as a child. There were times I'd be picking cotton and hear an old crop-duster coming. I couldn't help but stop what I was doing to watch it effortlessly gliding through the air. Dad wasn't nearly as enthralled with them as I was. "Get back to picking," he'd tell me when he saw me standing there engrossed and following the airplane to the horizon with my eyes.

I was 12 years old the first time I ever rode in an airplane. The old airport wasn't but a mile or so up the road from home, and a pilot there would give kids a ride for a dollar. It took a long time to save a hundred pennies, but when I finally did it, I was happy to relinquish my hard-earned money to that pilot for a chance to go up in the air. I don't guess it occurred to me then that I would ever fly one myself.

Learning to fly an airplane at first seemed secondary to all of the classes that were required in flight school. There was so much to learn. Our days were divided into two parts. First, we went to class, learned all about the airplane, studied the engine, the rules of the air and of flight, flight controls, and how we should conduct ourselves. I'll never forget the lesson that oil does not wear out, it only gets dirty.

In addition to that, there was the physical education they made us do. We played football, golf, and tennis, and we learned boxing and wrestling. Each officer was meant to be adept at many different sports.

In the second part of the day, we'd fly.

Our training was performed in a T-34 Mentor— a single-engine, tandem, two-seated aircraft. We called our instructor Smith. He only weighed about 120 pounds, but he was a good guy and everybody liked him. I had a tendency to be heavy-handed in my flying. Smith was always saying, "Dammit, Clemens, turn it loose. It flies better without you."

Nevertheless, after just 6.5 hours of flying with Smith onboard, it was time for me to take my first solo flight. I was nervous to be alone, even though all I had to do was take off, fly a little piece, and then come back and land. It was comforting to know that I had the instructor in my ear if I was to screw up.

After 30 hours in the T-34, it was time to train in a T-28. That was like going from a Pinto to a Cadillac. The T-28 was strong with a big engine. In it, we'd learn to fly by stalling, stall recovery, barrel rolls, loops, and Immelmann turns. Nervousness performing these maneuvers quickly wore off. Before long, we were doing vertical recoveries just for fun. To think that I once had to save my pennies for a quick ride on a little airplane, and now here I was flying for fun on the Air Force's dime.

There was a whole month when we could not fly much due to the bad weather. That made for the only time in my entire military career that I would not complete the four hours of flying that would earn me $125 in hazard pay.

When the first six months of flight training were over, we graduated to the next phase. Nearly 35 percent of the trainees did not finish because of their lack of skills, bad attitudes, or physical inabilities. As for those of us who were left, half of us would go to single-engine training and half would go to multi-engine training. I measured somewhere in the middle and was able to choose what type of advanced training I wanted to do. Taking my height and girth into account, I decided I would be more comfortable in multi-engines. And with that, it was time to say goodbye to Marianna and hello to San Angelo, Texas.

GOODFELLOW AIR FORCE BASE, SAN ANGELO, TEXAS. 1956-1957

The movers came and packed up our sparse belongings in the garage apartment we had rented in Marianna. Once again, Lil, Sue, and I hopped in the Oldsmobile and set forth for a new destination. This time we pointed ourselves west, to Goodfellow Air Force Base in San Angelo, Texas. It was 800 miles and two days of travel, but I didn't mind the time on the road because the government paid me for the move by the mile.

We found a nice apartment and were able to settle in immediately. San Angelo was a beautiful little city. The only bad thing was that it was in the middle of a seven-year drought. The dust storms that occurred there during this time rivaled those the country saw during the Dust Bowl of the 1930s. It was impossible to keep the dust out of the house, and Lil certainly hated it.

Ranchers and farmers throughout the whole state were hit hard by the scarcity of water and the increasing costs of feed. President Dwight D. Eisenhower visited San Angelo in January of 1957, where he launched his inspection tour of West Texas farms and ranches that had been affected by the drought. I guess it seemed like just about every cloud that rolled through was empty.

Just after Eisenhower left San Angelo, the sky opened up, and we saw an end to the drought, and in fact, a deluge of rainfall came over the next few months. If I learned one thing about rain growing up on a farm, it's that either there's never enough or there's enough to wash the fields away.

Drought or not, flood or not, I thought San Angelo was the best place we ever lived, because it was organized and offered a lot of support for families.

Flight training at Goodfellow was similar to what we had done in the first six months. This go around, we were training in a converted B-25 — a stripped-down, real 2-engine B-25 with nothing left but three seats in the cockpit. All of it was educational to this old country boy, especially the emphasis on instrument formation flying. That took a lot of our time in simulators and in the air. I still brag that I was probably the last pilot to pass an instrument check on the aural null navigation system. It was soon eliminated by the Vortex Navigation system. That upgrade in technology would make flying a lot easier, and it gave us the ability to make blind landings.

When flight training ended, I had to decide where my stretch in the Air Force would take me next, but first, I took my pilot's certification over to the FAA, and they awarded me a commercial pilot's certification that I would use in later years and could still use today if I passed the physical.

I had finished 12th out of a class of 120. I learned at Graham Air Base that class ranking matters. It gives you options. That's how I had the opportunity to choose to fly multi-engine planes. The guys who finished top of the class chose the Military Air Transport Service. What was left to choose from was a weather B-29, a seaplane, the KC-97, or the B-47. I'd heard about the B-47, and it seemed like a terrible assignment. It was a crappy airplane, one of the first big jet bombers we ever had. You still had to shoot the stars to navigate it.

Coincidentally, it was around this time that the Green Bay Packers sent me a contract and asked if I wanted to come back and play football, but since I had chosen to become a pilot, I was committed to the Air Force for four more years. It was no big loss. The professional football experience had been like going back to the damn dark ages, with the team's shoddy equipment and methods. I wouldn't have gone back even if I could have.

I decided my future would be on the KC-97. Hunter Air Force Base in Savannah, Georgia, needed co-pilots, and that would be my next duty station. The KC-97 was an airliner made by Boeing, but converted by the Air Force to be a fuel tanker. It had an entire crew and was big enough to be comfortable. Time would prove that I made the right decision. In the years to come, I will have the opportunity to visit some of my other options. Morocco, for example, had no officers' club and no PX. Just a chow hall and motor scooting, drag racing. Very boring.

My next stop was West Palm Beach Air Force Base for training on the KC-97.

WEST PALM BEACH, FLORIDA. AUGUST 1957

The Air Force hired movers to pack up our household goods and shipped them ahead of us to Savannah, since that would be my next duty station.

Lil, Sue, and I took the long way to West Palm and made a pit stop at both of our parents' homes for a short visit. The government was paying after all, and I always like to squeeze the dollars.

When we got to Florida, we found an apartment that was located only a block from the Atlantic Ocean for $60 a month. The three of us were such a novelty that the neighbors couldn't seem to do enough for our family— an Air Force pilot who'd once played for the Green Bay Packers, a beauty queen, and a one-year-old child. I don't know what it was, maybe they thought we were poor, but some of them even did our laundry for us.

For two months, I learned the ropes of the KC-97. The flight manual was 1.5 inches thick, and the instrument manual was about the same. I learned it all backwards and forwards. But every day when duty was over, my little family and I would head to the beach. I'd carry little Sue out into the water, and with my hands under her back, she'd float and look up happily at the sunny Florida sky as the soothing salt water waved over her little body. She just loved it.

It was hard to say goodbye to all of that after only two months, but military life isn't exactly known for fostering deep roots in any one place.

However, Savannah, Georgia, would become the home base for the next six years.

HUNTER AIR FORCE BASE, SAVANNAH, GEORGIA. SEPTEMBER 1957.

We arrived in Savannah on a Saturday. We were lucky to find a cheap two-bedroom apartment. Or so we thought. Come 5 a.m. Monday, we were startled awake as B-47s screamed over the rooftop of our home. We had not realized our apartment was located at the end of Hunter's runway. This unexpected pandemonium nearly scared Lil and me to death. As you can imagine, our one-year-old took the disturbance none too well, and she let us know of her disapproval by filling the air with cries almost as loud as the rumble from the plane's engines.

We were relieved to find out that the landlord understood our situation and would allow us to renege on our lease. We were able to find a house located away from base, and began to get settled into our new home and a new routine.

I checked in at the 308th Air Refueling Squadron with extremely limited knowledge of the squadron's mission — air refueling. I was in store for more education from the get-go.

In West Palm Beach, I had not been in charge of checking the airplane for bad tires, leaks in the wing, or dents. Now that I was a co-pilot, those pre-flight checks became my responsibility.

Most of the procedures were not difficult to learn. Strategic Air Command's (SAC) greatest emphasis was crew coordination. The success of our mission relied on our working well together to get the job done. That was tough for some of the guys who had piloted smaller planes all by themselves.

Me with my first crew in Savannah, Georgia.

Our six-man crew consisted of me, the pilot, a flight engineer, a navigator, a boom operator, and a radio operator. In our mission, we had to successfully communicate not just among ourselves, but with the FAA, air controllers, and the airplane that was set to receive the fuel.

The aircraft commander and I had to attend scheduled simulator training in Delaware and Tampa, in addition to our training at Hunter. This is how we learned how to respond in emergency situations. We were trained in procedures of both the SAC and Boeing.

My aircraft commander was like a little banty rooster, always picking fights with people bigger than him that he didn't have a snowball's chance in hell of whipping up on. It became customary on these TDYs for me to have to rescue my 120-pound superior.

Another of my responsibilities was keeping up with all the communication manuals of the entire United States, along with the aircraft manuals for myself and the pilot. Part of that included maps for all over the country, because you never know where you're going to have to go. It took both hands for me to carry all of them.

In addition to that, I was given the duty of serving as the Ground Refueling Officer and the CBR officer. As the Ground Refueling Officer, I was responsible for supervising the refueling of our aircraft. As the CBR officer — Chemical, Biological, and Radiological — I was tasked with reading other crew members' disseminator indicators. The indicators were worn around their necks with their dog tags, and if they had been exposed to chemical radiation, I could tell by looking at the tag. This was an important job because the gas in some of the bombs could have killed you if you were exposed. Luckily, no one was contaminated while I was a CBR officer.

After a month of training in Savannah, I was officially qualified as a KC-97 combat co-pilot on a combat crew. None of us were foot soldiers anymore. We were SAC's finest ... the sky kings. Everybody did everything for us. Some people joke that I still expect that of people today, but it's the truth. We were the sky kings.

On October 30, my second daughter was born. We named her Sharon. You might say it was a busy time at home with two babies and a new job. Lil and I were lucky to have our mothers, who came to help minimize the chaos. My work hours were crazy, and it was a tough time. But we managed.

AZORES ISLANDS. 1958

In March of 1958, my squadron was deployed for three months to the Lajes Field Air Force Base, which is located on the Azores Islands in Portugal. Our operation mostly consisted of flying three-hour missions out and three hours back to the Air Force Base that we shared with the Portuguese Air Force. In the pre-jet age, this was a refueling stop for all aircraft flying to and from Europe.

One of the perks of being on the KC-97 crew was that we could bring along our motorbikes and scooters since there was room on our plane for them. That meant whenever we had free time, we had transportation so we could find something to fill our time. One of the best short getaways for those of us who golfed was the 18-hole golf course located about five miles from the airbase. We'd just hop on our motor scooters and make the ten-minute trip down the road. The cost was one cent per hole, plus one cent per hole for the caddy. The only problem was that the farmers let their cattle graze on the golf course grass at night. This caused more than one of us to find an unplayable lie.

One evening, I was lucky enough to be invited to a formal banquet at the Portuguese Air Base Officers' Club. I put on my dress uniform and was happy to attend their celebration. It was an exquisite ballroom where a fabulous nine-course meal was served. Thanks to my fraternity days, I knew just which fork to use and when. The silverware, china, and crystal were the finest I'd ever seen. The meal included wine, and all it cost me was seven cents. That was a pretty cheap night on the town, and an amazing thing to experience.

The islands were located about two-thirds of the way to Europe, and a lot of our R&R time, between missions, was spent exploring different European countries.

During our three-month tour, I took two trips to England for a long weekend. I visited London during my first trip. We landed at daybreak and took a train into the city. When we arrived at Paddington Station, I noticed that at least half of the men there had a leg or an arm, or sometimes both, missing. I could only assume these were injuries sustained during World War II.

We stayed at the Columbia House Officers' Club for two nights. At that time, the exchange rate was not in our favor, and a pound cost $2.25 in American currency. Because of that, we rode the underground train to see the sights. We saw the changing of the guard, Big Ben, the cathedrals, and a six-block yard sale, where I bought a set of expensive China for about 1/4 of what it would have cost back home.

The last two weeks of our tour were spent in Sidi Slimane, Morocco. One night when we had nothing better to do, my other crew members and I loaded up our station wagon and drove to the nearest resort town. Something I will never forget from that night is the image of our radio operator asking a local cop how to get to the "house of ill repute." He got the job because the radio operator is the low man on the totem pole. Since our radio operator didn't speak Arabic, he used hand signals to get the directions. I guess some signals look the same in any language because the cop pointed us in the right direction. We only wanted to see what the African babes looked like. It didn't look inviting, and none of the crew were inclined to stay.

Just before it was time to head back to Savannah, I had three days of leave that I could either take or lose. I decided to catch a ride to Nouasseur Air Base— a former US Air Force Strategic Air Command Base just outside of Casablanca.

The next day, I decided I wanted to see what the Atlantic Ocean looked like from Africa. I hired a taxi to take me there, and when I reached it, I had to look down at the water from a high wall, but no one was playing on the beach like I had with my family when we lived on the other side of the same ocean. The view was beautiful, though.

A Moroccan bus was the only way to get back to Sidi Slimane. The top of the bus was loaded with chickens, ducks, goats, dogs, and any other animal you could imagine. I was ever so happy to arrive back at Sidi Slimane.

When my time there was almost up, I made a deal with a fellow service member to take his three dogs back to the States for him for $75 each. There was plenty of room for the animals on our KC-97, and I'm always up for making extra cash. The look on Lil's face when I walked off the plane with three dogs was priceless. I guess she thought I had brought her a few pets, but they stayed with a veterinarian until their owners came home.

After three months away, I was happy to be back home with all of my girls. Homecoming was great with Lil. A little too great. Surprise! Pregnant again.

ALERT AT DOW AIR FORCE BASE. BANGOR, MAINE 1958

I had a few quiet months back in Savannah before things got busy again. In the fall of 1958, I traveled to DOW Air Force Base in Bangor, Maine, for my first experience being on alert.

When you're on alert duty, there's not much you can do. You have to be combat-ready on a moment's notice in case anything should happen. The United States had been in an arms race with Russia for some time, so for years, anytime the Soviets deployed, our military went on alert.

The purpose of our squadron's rotation at DOW was so that we could be positioned north in order to act expediently in case of a nuclear attack. Our mission was to refuel bombers on their way to drop a nuke on the USSR, but we never got shot at. The Russians knew they couldn't whip us. We were a deterrent force.

Though we would have alert duty on and off for years to come, this was the first time being on alert for tanker crews. There was a lot of confusion about our restrictions. We only knew what we had heard from the B-47 crews, who had been on alert in England and Morocco. In the beginning, we at least had access to a station wagon. It didn't last very long because someone got intoxicated and wrecked it. Probably wrecked their career too.

You could not leave base while on alert, so my activities were limited to shopping at the PX or visiting the Officers' Club.

The weather in Maine was much different from what I was used to, having lived in the Southeast for most of my life. One day, I took a walk to the PX. It was a nice sunny day when I entered the store. After about 30 minutes, I came out to find that it was snowing and the wind was blowing about 40 miles per hour. There I was in my summer clothes. That taught me never to go anywhere without a jacket.

When we were getting ready to depart for Savannah after our first alert duty was over, I witnessed a single jet engine plane do a landing in the negative degree snowy windy weather. I never dreaded another kind of weather takeoff or landing the rest of my career, because if that pilot could make that kind of landing all alone, then surely I could handle anything with an entire crew.

Alert duty lasted anywhere from a week to two weeks at a time, and then we'd fly back home, and there would be other missions for SAC and time to spend with family.

Something happened on one mission that would hamper my full enjoyment of coffee for the rest of my life. We were on an eight-hour flight, and it was nearing 3 a.m. I asked the boom operator to fix me a cup, and told him I liked mine with cream and sugar. I was standing near the galley and looked back to see him searching for a spoon to stir in the cream and sugar. When he couldn't find one, he used the nearest thing he could find— a screwdriver with no telling what on it. I never ordered anything extra in my coffee for the next twenty years of my flying career, and to this day, I drink my coffee black.

1959: CHANGES IN OUR FAMILY

The 1950s had truly been a wild ride. In just ten short years, I had gone from being president of my high school class to an all-star football player for the University of Georgia, to a husband and father, to a professional football player, to a junior high teacher and basketball coach, to an Air Force pilot. It was an exciting decade by anyone's measure.

During 1959, I continued my refueling missions and alert duties with Strategic Air Command. I was away from home nearly two weeks out of every two months, and my youngest daughter, Dawn, was born in March. She came early, just like Sue had. And I missed her birth just like I had Sue's. Missing important events and milestones is just a part of military life. We had to accept it and adapt. Adapting doesn't always make it easier, but it does make homecomings that much more special.

The birth of Dawn meant Lil was juggling three young children at home while I was away. Sue was getting older, almost six now. Her body grew big, strong, and healthy, but her mental handicaps were not improving. Her needs became unmanageable at home because she required total supervision almost 24 hours a day to keep her from wandering off or getting injured.

She had been attending an institution that served children with disabilities called Kicklighter School. Lil served as its director, and I volunteered some of my free time there doing things like painting and mowing the grass. But that year, we made the difficult decision to send Sue to live at Gracewood— a hospital in Augusta for people with developmental disabilities. It wasn't easy to see Sue sent to live away from home, but we knew Gracewood had the capacity to give her far better care than we could. She stayed there until she was nearly a teenager, and we visited and volunteered there often.

1960: A NEW DECADE

In 1959, I had declined an offer to accept a regular commission with the Air Force. It would have required me to serve until retirement. With only four years of service under my belt, I wanted to keep my options open and maintain the ability to say whether or not I extended my time with the Air Force at any given time.

My intentions had been to leave the service and fly commercially. I had a connection at Delta Airlines who could have gotten me a job. But when my five-year commitment was up on September 19, 1960, I decided to stay in the Air Force.

To be honest, Lil really didn't take too kindly to the idea of me traveling the world with all of those stewardesses, and with three children to take care of, it would have been hard for us to give up the healthcare benefits we received with the Air Force.

Besides all that, I enjoyed the lifestyle. I made enough money to live, and I got to travel all over the country on the Air Force's dime. I was in the groove of military life, and I adapted to being away from home often.

Even though I continued my career with the Air Force, I never accepted a regular commission and remained a reserve member for as long as I served. I never wanted to give up my option to become a civilian in case something better was to come along, but it never did.

I wondered if being in the Air Force Reserve might hinder my promotions, but throughout the years, that never seemed to be the case. Besides the fact that I was very efficient at all of my jobs, I thought it never hurt anything that the higher-ups seemed to like me. Throughout my career, they would request me to be their co-pilot when they put in their four hours for flight pay. They always liked me, I think, because I'd do all the work of the pilot and co-pilot. All they had to do was sit back and "drive." I even did a lot of hours with Col. Thomas Ferebee, the Enola Gay bombardier who had dropped the first atomic bomb on Hiroshima in 1945.

1960 was a remarkably busy year. My squadron's alert was moved to Newfoundland. The weather there might have been warmer than in Maine, but there was a hell of a lot more snow. The cheap booze and delicious French pastries made up for it, though. I played a lot of bridge and poker there when it was cold, and in the summer, we would hold softball games on the concrete aircraft ramp. I even hit a mile and a half home run once and had to take the alert truck to retrieve the ball.

After a month of alert in Newfoundland, the Air Force decided I needed more training as an officer and sent me on a three-month assignment to Squadron Officer's School at Maxwell Air Force Base in Montgomery. There were 12 students assigned to one instructor there, and the subjects covered all aspects of the United States government and the United States Air Force. We also had to participate in athletics, which included soccer, volleyball, and touch football. Most of my classmates were lieutenants, but there were a few captains.

While I was getting more officer training, Lil was busy training to be a beauty queen. She entered the Mrs. Georgia pageant and won. The contest was judged partly on homemaking capabilities, and Lil was required to bake a cake, prepare a chilled refrigerator dessert, and cook her favorite casserole dish all in two hours. As far as I was concerned, she couldn't even make a biscuit. I do seem to recall having to eat a lot of chicken while she practiced her recipes. Either her cooking improved, or her good looks and other skills counted for a whole lot, because she won the whole shebang. She earned the title of Mrs. Georgia, a free summer wardrobe, a silver bowl, and a hundred-dollar savings bond. She was also given the opportunity to buy a dishwasher at cost, which she jumped at because she hated washing dishes.

After that, she was headed to Fort Lauderdale to compete in the Mrs. America contest.

The Air Force allowed me to leave Montgomery and travel to Fort Lauderdale so I could escort Lil in the pageant. I hired a student from Homestead Air Force Base flying club to fly me, and all I had to pay for was gas.

A newspaper report from The Atlanta Journal said Lil was a picture of good grooming, poise, and glowing personality. That wasn't enough to win her the crown, which was a shame, because first prize that year was a brand new house in Fort Lauderdale.

Defeated by Mrs. Indiana and Mrs. Minnesota, Lil placed second runner-up. Out of 51 contestants, that wasn't too shabby for a 26-year-old mother who had a hard time cooking a large meal at home. She won a silver tray, a refrigerator, a year's supply of beauty products, and 250 square feet of floor tile. I was proud of her, but when you're married with three kids, it's a pat on the butt and back to work. She had her thing, and I had mine, really.

When I got back to Maxwell, I needed to get in my four hours of flying time so I could receive my flight pay for the month. There was a squadron of C-47s, which were big, heavy planes, and that's what we flew to get our hours in. I showed up at the assigned time and located the other two pilots assigned to fly it, and since we had already heard how hard it was to land a C-47, we flipped a coin to see which one of us would do it. I won the toss.

After four hours of flying, it was time to land. Neither I nor the other pilots had ever landed a tail-wheel aircraft, but we talked it over and said a little prayer as we started our descent. The final approach was standard, but the landing and rollout were all new. Luckily, we survived with a little help from the crew chief. I only repeated this experience once, and I wouldn't have done it if I hadn't needed my $125.00 flight pay.

After Maxwell, I was back home at Hunter Air Force Base for about a month when I was selected to upgrade to aircraft commander in the

KC-97. That meant I had to report to Randolph Air Force Base in Texas for two months of training in the captain's seat.

Since Lil required the Oldsmobile to transport herself and the children around, I had to find a way to get myself to Texas. I figured I could buy a car, put it on payments, make one payment, and then sell it as soon as I got back to Georgia, so I wouldn't have to make a second payment.

I don't remember what kind of vehicle it was, but it got me to Texas. I was even able to stop in Scottsboro to visit Mom and Dad for a day. I didn't get home much during my military career. Mom would visit us, but Dad wouldn't leave the farm long enough. It was nice to have the opportunity for a short visit, especially since I didn't have time to help with farm chores.

The school at Randolph was easy, and the time was pleasant because one of my college classmates was in the same class as me. After graduation, I was a KC-97 F or G Aircraft Commander. I would now be the boss of the aircraft and the crew, but being an Aircraft Commander came with added responsibility. I was now responsible for whatever aircraft I was flying. Still, it felt good to know I'd be in the captain's seat.

I drove back to Hunter and knew I needed to quickly unload the vehicle I had purchased before the time came to make the next payment. I noticed it was leaking some kind of red oil on the driveway, and I soon discovered a transmission leak. There goes my plan, I thought. But I asked one of the flight engineers how I could fix the car without replacing the transmission, and he told me to drain all the fluids, wipe the case clean, and spread a compound around the edge of the pan. Then I needed to let it sit for a few days to see if that does the trick. In the meantime, I advertised the car for sale. In just two days, I found a buyer. During the closing of the sale at the bank, I learned that the buyer had recently been in prison, and he was currently working as a tombstone salesman. What a combination. As I cashed the check, I wondered what he would do if I had sold him a lemon, but figured that was good riddance. I had my money, and he had the title. I never heard from him, so I guess the seal job was successful.

When I returned to work as a new aircraft commander, I was assigned a young crew, which consisted of 2nd lieutenants and staff sergeants. My co-pilot was also an aeronautical engineer. The rest of the year was full of changes.

As reciprocating aircraft were being phased out, the 308th Bomb Wing, which I belonged to, was deactivated. That meant that most crews and support personnel had to transfer to the 2nd Bomb Wing or to another base. Earlier manufactured B-47s and KC-97s were flown to the bone yard in Tucson, Arizona, and laid to rest in the desert where the air was dry.

My crew transferred to the 2nd Air Refueling Squadron of the Second Bomb Wing, and we still went to Newfoundland for alert duty two weeks out of every two months. Typically, we knew our schedules well ahead of time and made our plans accordingly. So for Christmas that year, Lil and I planned to take the girls to visit both of our parents.

Unfortunately, another aircraft commander's son got into some legal trouble and spoiled my family's holiday plans. I was a new AC and still low man on the totem pole. That meant I had to take his place in Newfoundland for Christmas.

I wasn't happy to be leaving my family over the holidays, but I didn't know I was in store for a fun Christmas away from home. Unbeknownst to me, Bob Hope was set to perform his Christmas show at the Ernest Harmon Air Base that year. The show was held in a large maintenance building, and my crew was given prime seating near the center stage. The show was performed on Christmas Eve, and the next day at lunch, I had the honor of dining across the table from Bob Hope, Jane Mansfield, and Anita Bryant. Bob Hope was a funny guy, and I didn't mind Jane Mansfield sitting across from me in her tight sweater either. Being on alert duty during Christmas wasn't so bad after all, and I had a good story to tell when I got home.

TROUBLE BREWING IN CUBA

Life rocked on as usual for a while, with refueling missions, alert in Newfoundland, and time with family when I was able to be home. But 1962 would bring change to our routine.

When Fidel Castro's regime severed Cuba's ties with the United States and hopped into bed with the Soviet Union, it changed the way the US guarded itself against nuclear attack. After the Bay of Pigs invasion failed to overthrow Castro in 1961, he made a secret agreement with Soviet Premier Nikita Khrushchev to place nuclear missiles in Cuba. We'd spent years being combat-ready and serving on alert duty in the Northeast, but now the Soviets had armed an ally in close proximity to the Southeast United States.

Time was spent moving equipment, airplanes, and crews in and out of the Southeast. Our bombers were dispersed to civilian airports throughout the region so that the Russians would have more targets than they had missiles. KC-97s were used in support of these missions since they had ample cargo space.

On one trip to MacDill Air Force Base in Florida, my crew unloaded support items for the build-up, including Army equipment. When it was time for us to depart, there was so much equipment staging around the runway that the only place I could find to turn the plane around was a large hangar. It was strange driving and turning around and out of a hangar in a large cargo aircraft. But we did what we had to do.

The Strategic Air Command was responsible for the aerial photography of the missile buildup in Cuba, and therefore, it was also responsible for refueling the reconnaissance aircraft, which were stationed in the Midwest.

Our refueling track was about 100 miles south of New Orleans. The RB-47s would exit Cuba, climb to high altitude, and meet the tanker for fuel to continue their missions back to the Midwest. On one mission, we arrived at the refueling location around dusk, and thunderstorms surrounded the area. As we waited for the RB-47 to arrive and take on fuel, our number three engine failed. We were at 15,000 feet, but had to descend to 8,000 feet to maintain flight level.

To further complicate things, the RB-47 was late. Procedures were to proceed to the nearest United States Air Force base and land, but we waited for thirty minutes in case he showed up. Finally, through a small break in the clouds, we saw a contrail from a jet aircraft coming our way. Just then, the RB-47 called us. He was there and ready to take on fuel.

I explained the situation. We could only give him 20,000 pounds of fuel, and he would have to get down to 7,000 feet since we had lost the number three engine and couldn't get up to the usual refueling altitude. He said he thought he could do it. Despite the circumstances, we were able to complete the offload of fuel as an electrical storm surged all around us. The RB-47 made its way back to the Midwest, where all the data it had recorded would be processed and studied.

We were supposed to land at the closest airport, but we decided we could make it back to Turner. Before we were set to land, I let them know that we had lost an engine, and upon landing, we were met with firetrucks and all sorts of crazy stuff.

The next day, we were informed that we had to fly to the Lajes Field in the Azores for alert duty. Nuclear missile sites had been photographed in Cuba, and the Strategic Air Command was ordered to DEFCON 2. It looked like the Cold War might be heating up. This was especially scary because if Cuba launched missiles, our families in Savannah were well within striking range.

Our crew, maintenance personnel, and supplies left for the Azores less than 24 hours after we had refueled the RB-47 with an engine down and lightning striking all around us. We flew to Charleston, then to Bermuda, and then to the Azores. After 12 hours, we finally landed, were assigned quarters, and were briefed on our mission.

My crew would be on alert for two days, have one day off, and then repeat. When we were on alert, we would spend two days in a maintenance hangar on three-story cots. Each time the two days rolled around, it seemed like a lifetime before the day off would come, and the one day off was always over in the blink of an eye. But since I had been at Lages a few years earlier, I knew about the golf course and a few other sights that were nice to visit. We would often spend that off day riding scooters to and from the golf course, and the cost of 18 cents for 18 holes was the same as it had been in 1958.

Tensions mounted for several weeks, but finally the Cuban Missile Crisis came to an end when the US agreed to remove its missiles from Turkey and the Soviets began shipping their missiles back to the Soviet Union. My crew was able to head back home to Savannah pretty soon after that. The return flight was 4,000 feet, and it took 16 hours of flight time.

Throughout 1962, my crew had been training for the Strategic Air Command Bomb Competition— a competition held each year to inspire crews and help bomber units improve their bombing accuracy. We were the youngest crew in the SAC to have been chosen. All of our competition training turned out to be for nothing, because the competition got cancelled due to everything going on in Cuba that year. Still, it was an immense honor to have been chosen for the competition in the first place.

In the midst of everything going on in the world, I earned my 1500-hour wings and made the rank of captain. It had been a long and eventful year.

HUNTER AIR FORCE BASE CLOSES

t the end of 1962, rumors started swirling that Hunter would be placed on the closing list. In 1963, rumors turned to truth. Hunter Air Force Base would be closed by 1964. On top of that, the KC-97s would be phased out. We were entering the jet age. That meant that I would be training to fly the KC-135 Stratotanker. It also meant that our crews would become smaller, since the co-pilot would be able to act in the capacity of the flight engineer on the new planes.

My crew flew three KC-97s to the boneyard in Arizona and rode back on a commercial airline each time. One of the strange things I remember is that we flew back to Savannah on Southern Airways or Delta in a tail dragger aircraft, which meant we entered and exited through a door located just forward of the plane's tail.

I left Hunter in 1963. Strategic Air Command assigned me to Turner Air Force Base in Albany, which, as luck would have it, was only 50 miles away from Lil's hometown of Blakely.

One of the downsides of leaving Savannah was that we would have to leave our maid, Pearlie, behind. She was a 40-year-old woman who'd ride the bus every day to the main gate of the base, where we would pick her up. We paid her bus fare and gave her a dollar a day for housekeeping and babysitting. We loved her and she loved us. I became Pearlie's hero after a Yankee lawyer from New Jersey tried to swindle her out of $1,000 that was owed to her from an insurance policy refund. I took the matter to some of the Air Force lawyers, and we got Pearlie's money. My stock went way up with her after that. It was sad for the entire family when we had to tell her goodbye.

Training for the KC-135 began in Reno, Nevada. Lil and the kids took the Oldsmobile and spent that time with her parents in Blakely, and I bought a Fiat Spider and made my way to the mountains for survival training.

I don't mind telling you, survival training was pure hell. This particular training was meant to help us should we ever become a Russian prisoner of war. On a cold, snowy, and sleety night, we had to crawl into a field where we ventured through rope and mud courses with machine guns shooting over our heads. Finally, we were captured by pseudo Russians and put in a Stalag. We couldn't sit down, and we couldn't stand up all the way, and they would take us out one by one for interrogation. They didn't beat us or anything, but they messed with our minds. I was happy to have that part of the training behind me, and luckily, I never had to put any of it to use.

The next stop was California, where we would learn the ins and outs of the KC-135.

After all of the simulator and academic training, I was assigned to train with a complete crew that would be assigned to a base in Oklahoma. In other words, I was an outsider since I was only a substitute member of the crew. In local terms, I was the bastard AC. I shared time in the pilot position for half of the training, which included take-offs, landings, air refueling bombers, and air refueling fighter aircraft.

During my last two weeks in California, Lil left the girls with her parents and flew out to spend two weeks with me. I was able to find us a small apartment for the duration of her stay. It was not our dream getaway, by any means. In fact, it was downright bad, but I returned to the same apartment in 1970, and the 1963 version was the Taj Mahal compared to what I saw when I went back.

When training ended, Lil and I drove back to Georgia in my little convertible. The first stop of our road trip was Las Vegas. We had dinner and saw a show. Since both of us were still wide awake, we decided to drive a little further down the road. Around four in the morning, we stopped in Arizona. We slept there until noon, and then we drove to President George Bush's hometown of Odessa in Texas. We stayed the night there, and our next stop was Blakely. We didn't make it back until late that night, and our girls were already fast asleep. It was a big surprise when they woke up the next morning and found us there. It was a great homecoming.

We spent another day in Blakely, and then it was time to find a new place to live in Albany. We meant to rent, but all of the places were terrible, so we decided to purchase a new house. It was located thirty minutes across town from Turner. I had gotten rid of the Fiat because it burned a lot of oil, and after I replaced the rings on the cylinders, I never trusted it. I was back to driving the Oldsmobile, and it burned a lot of gas. It only took us a year to get tired of that commute before we sold the house and signed up for base housing. We were assigned a three-bedroom house near the main base and were able to sell the house without a loss. And Mom and Dad gave me their "fishing car" to replace my Fiat. It was a 1957 four-door Chevrolet, and I had to replace almost all of the interior.

When I reported to my new squadron at Turner, I found that two of my college Air Force ROTC fellows were there. Despite our common background, I did not get a warm welcome. They were co-pilots and still in the Aircraft Commander upgrade program. The commander of the squadron put me in the upgrade program even though I was already an AC. When SAC found out, the squadron was forced to assign me to a crew as Aircraft Commander. This made the commander mad. He felt like I'd jumped ahead of his favorite guys, but I couldn't help that I came to Turner already an AC. He never warmed up to me in the three years I was there, but I didn't give a damn if anyone liked me or not. I did my job.

OPERATION CHROME DOME

Since 1961, Strategic Air Command had placed B-52s armed with thermonuclear missiles on continuous airborne alert. The B-52s would fly for 24 hours at a time to ensure that the United States could quickly respond should the Soviets attack.

Due to a shortage of pilots on the B-52s in 1965, pilots from the KC-135 squadrons were designated as third pilots on those 24-hour flights. Since I was an aircraft commander, I was selected to be the third pilot on these missions, not once, but twice.

My duty was to sit in one of the pilot seats so one of the other two pilots could get sleep on the flight. While he rested, I monitored the instruments and did whatever the other pilot asked me to do.

The mission was long, and the route was interesting. We took off and headed to the North Pole, then we turned southeast over Greenland and coasted into the western end of the Mediterranean Sea. As we approached the Mediterranean Sea, we contacted the awaiting tanker and rendezvoused with it to unload about 130,000 pounds of fuel, which is about 22,000 gallons. After refueling, we continued to the east end of the Mediterranean and circled back to the west and circled again.

There was only one place in the B-52 that one could stand up straight, and that was the steps from the lower deck to the upper deck. The navigator and the bomb navigator were downstairs. The AC, co-pilot, and electronic warfare officer were upstairs with the tail gunner in the tail of the aircraft. There was room on the upper deck for two crew members to lie on a sleeping bag, and if you needed to pee, you had to do it in a can.

Needless to say, twenty-four hours was a long time to spend on a B-52, especially if you couldn't sleep.

After my first 24-hour flight with the B-52 guys, I remembered why I was so glad I was able to fly a tanker. B-52s fly all over the world and then end up right back where they started. On a tanker, you go to different places and actually get to step off the plane sometimes.

MY FIRST TOUR IN VIETNAM

In March of 1966, the 2nd Bomb Wing at Turner Air Force Base was ordered to Southeast Asia to support the war effort in Vietnam.

All personnel, aircraft, and supplies were to serve for six months. This would be my first time working in a combat zone, and I was required to get my affairs in order in case I didn't make it back. That's what we all were supposed to do, but one guy got caught slacking. We were ready to take off for our deployment when a general on the runway started waving his hand to stop us. Turned out one of the guys going over with us hadn't left his wife a dime. I guess he was pretty embarrassed as he slid past the other 79 people onboard the plane to give his wife some money. What a send-off!

While the B-52s headed nonstop to Guam, the KC-135s carried personnel and equipment for the wing. The goal was to move three tankers per day. We'd make a stop in California to pick up supplies and let the crews rest, and then fly to Hawaii for refueling and crew change.

My crew had rested in Hawaii overnight. I remember sitting at the back of the Hickman Officer's Club, sipping a mai tai and watching the Navy's large ships and submarines entering and leaving Pearl Harbor. That was a really interesting sight to take in while I waited for the next KC-135 to come so we could head to Southeast Asia.

I didn't have much time for sightseeing, but my co-pilot, Baron, was a Mormon, and I went with him to see the Honolulu Stake Mormon Tabernacle. He could have gone in if he wanted to, but since I wasn't allowed, he didn't. We also happened to be at the Officers' Club when the officers'

My Young Tigers Tass Force patch.

wives were putting on a fashion show. It would have been considered risqué in the States, but I guess it was a pretty good send-off since we would be off to support the war in Vietnam in just a few hours.

The short stay in paradise ended, and we headed to Guam to drop off B-52 maintenance personnel and supplies. Our next stop was Kadena Air Force Base in Okinawa, Japan. That would be our home base for the next six months.

Tanker crews, given the code name "Young Tigers" during Vietnam, had proven themselves to be an indispensable part of the war. They allowed B-52s to travel longer ranges, and more than 500 times, they came to the rescue of a fighter or bomber who was a long way from his home base and found himself in desperate need of fuel. There's no telling how many bailouts were prevented thanks to the help of KC-135 crews. It has been said that the Young Tigers are some of the forgotten heroes of the war, and it's true that we didn't get much credit for what we did. To me, it felt like the B-52's got all the charm, and we got all the BS. But our life was a hell of a lot better than theirs, and I was thankful for that.

After arriving at Kadena, we were assigned to live in the Bachelor Officer Quarters, two to a room. I shared a room with my co-pilot. There was no air conditioning, and the quarters were located close to the main gate. All the noise made it hard to sleep during the day, but since most of our missions were flown at night, we did the best we could to rest.

My crew landed one day ahead of the first typhoon of the season, but before we could hunker down, we had to take on an Organization Readiness Inspection. We passed inspection and braced to experience our first typhoon. It turned out to be a false alarm, but since our tour was during typhoon season, it wasn't the last weather event we would encounter. Most of the time, we flew out and headed for the Philippines or Thailand before the bad ones hit. The rain did make for some hard times while we were there, though. I also experienced my first earthquake while stationed at Kadena. We were sitting on a rock, basically, so you can imagine what it felt like when everything started shaking. It was a weird feeling.

When the clouds lifted and the typhoon warning ended, my crew prepared for its first combat mission flight. We were told to fly over Vietnam and refuel four F-4s over Laos. Our flight time was meant to be four hours, over the course of which we would cross three time zones.

On the way over to Laos, our right-side hydraulic system failed. I reviewed the procedures and decided we could continue the mission by isolating the system. The problem with losing the right hydraulic system was that the boom refueling system worked off the right hydraulics. However, by using the current procedures, we could cross over the refueling system to the left hydraulic system and refuel the F-4s as planned.

At that time, the lowest altitude we could cross Vietnam at was 35,000 feet, but the refueling altitude for the flight of F-4s was 29,000 feet. Thus, we had to descend 11,000 feet after we passed Vietnam. The F-4s arrived on time, and we offloaded the fuel without any hiccups. After the refueling was completed, we isolated the right hydraulic system again and began making our way back to Kadena. The flight back was uneventful, but when we arrived, we found that the airfield was closed because the crosswinds were so high.

Our alternate airfield was Clark Air Force Base in the Philippines, which was an hour away. As bad luck would have it, we were about midway there when the left hydraulic system failed, too. And that was a huge problem. It compromised over half of our flight controls and landing gear, including the flaps, speed brakes, and our antilock brakes. That, on top of the fact that we were landing at a strange airfield and had limited flight time, because we had been in the air for 10 hours and didn't have much fuel left, meant that our luck would need to turn around if we had any chance of avoiding a crash.

There I was, left with nothing but emergency brakes for the landing.

On descent, the crew manually cranked the main gear down. It took 360 turns to fully crank the gear down, and then they had to manually turn the wing flaps down as well. It kind of reminded me of being back on the farm in the days before tractor equipment had any hydraulics. Hard work and muscle were all we had back then, and it's pretty much all we had to rely on in our aircraft that day.

As I attempted to land, facing cross winds that were as high as 10 knots, I had to keep the left wing down to maintain runway direction. Because we lost our anti-lock brakes, the two left outside tires locked as soon as they touched the runway. They exploded almost immediately, but with all of the excitement going on, I never even knew it. Thankfully, the aircraft was light enough that the two inside wheels were able to provide braking and load bearing. I used brakes to maintain direction, and brakes to turn off the runway, and finally, the engines were stopped, and we could breathe again. Our plane was towed to the ramp, and I was surprised to see the two wheels that had exploded.

We easily could have run off the end of the runway, and someone who didn't know what they were doing probably would have. Thankfully, I knew how to handle the situation, and with the help of my crew, we came out unscathed.

Twenty other aircraft were set to land at Clark Field that night, so they asked me to help find quarters for all of the crews. I finally got to my own quarters around 3 a.m. after I got everyone else bedded down.

At 8 a.m. the next morning, a tanker with a hydraulic specialist crew arrived with two wheels and four hydraulic pumps for my KC-135. They repaired everything, and my crew departed for Kadena at 4 p.m.

It was Friday, and we arrived back on base just in time for happy hour at the Officer's Club. After such an eventful first mission, we enjoyed the free drinks, food, and slot machines.

TAKHLI AIR FORCE BASE, THAILAND

After a few gaggles refueling the B-52s and returning to Kadena, we flew a mission to the war zone in Vietnam and then recovered to Takhli Air Force Base in Thailand. We would stay and fly combat missions from there for the next three weeks. Our mission was to refuel fighters that were bombing over Vietnam, as well as reconnaissance aircraft.

The facilities at Takhli were lacking, but we survived. We slept in a hootch, which was an individual building with a tin roof and a boarded walkway that led to toilets, showers, and other facilities. We shared it with the F-105 fighter pilot wing and EB-66 crews. The only air-conditioned place around was the bar, so naturally it was crowded every night of the week until 1 a.m.

It rained every afternoon we were there. We got so accustomed to it that we could set our clock by it. 4 o'clock and the rain starts, and it doesn't let up until the sun goes down. Another first was that we had to carry a flashlight with us everywhere we went at night, because of the many banded krait snakes. American GIs nicknamed it the "two-step snake," because if it bit you, you'd be dead in two steps.

Luckily, I never encountered one in the wild. I did, however, catch a glimpse of one at a local fair. They had a show where they pitted the snake against a sea bird. The bird would have to get hold of the snake before it bit him. I watched for about ten minutes, and it seemed the snake wasn't very aggressive and the bird wasn't hungry, because nothing happened, and I got bored and left. Everybody else seemed to think it was exciting,

Me standing outside a hootch in Thailand.

but I guess I preferred those cock fights I used to sneak and watch back in Alabama when I was a kid.

One day, after we had completed a mission, the base commander came to my building and asked my crew to fly a KC-135 back to Kadena. An EB-66 was inbound, and there was nowhere on the base to park it.

We packed up our clothes and gear, and they transported us to the airplane. It was about three in the afternoon, and the aircraft was closed up and hot as fire. When the crew chief opened the entrance, the inside of the plane must have been close to 150 degrees. After I made it to my seat, the temperature was only 135 degrees, but it could still smother you half to death. In order to be able to complete our pre-flight inspection, we all had to put on our oxygen masks and wear them at 100 percent oxygen. That was a miserable and fast pre-flight. Thirty minutes later, away we went. And just as we took off, there came the EB-66 on his final approach. Perfect timing. It took two hours of the three-hour flight to cool the interior of the craft. Talk about miserable.

Back at Kadena, my crew refueled B-52s for a while, but it wasn't long before we were assigned to Takhli again.

One F-105 pilot stationed there, Tony, had been a football teammate and a member of my Air Force ROTC squadron back at the University of Georgia. It was nice to be able to catch up with him, and it was interesting to hear about how he had survived bailing out of an F-105, which was so fast they could fly more than 1300 miles per hour. A lot of them were lost during the war because they flew dangerous missions. I guess my friend was lucky to have survived.

It was always interesting to run into someone I knew or had a connection to from back home while I was deployed. Another time, I was in line at the chow hall when I started making conversation with a staff sergeant. I asked him where he was from. "Hollywood," he told me. "Oh, California. I bet that's nice," I replied. "No, Alabama," he told me. It must truly be a small world, because Hollywood is only a little way down the road from my own hometown. I went on to find out that his uncle had worked on Dad's farm driving a tractor.

This time around at Takhli, things were easier because we knew the procedures and the area. Almost every day, we flew missions either over Laos or the Gulf of Tonkin. Each flight contained three tankers and 12 fighter-bomber aircraft. From the lead of the flight, it was a beautiful sight to see all the aircraft, except the tankers, turn towards their targets in North Vietnam. Some of the tankers loitered in case a fighter or bomber needed assistance with fuel, communication, or rescue recovery. The others flew back to recover at Takhli or Kadena.

On a day when we did not have a mission to fly, my navigator and I decided to take a train to Bangkok for dinner. There were more than 500 restaurants to choose from, and we picked a place that served Chinese food. The food was delicious.

Back at Takhli, my flying hours were approaching 120, which was the maximum allowed. Therefore, my crew was sent to Guam to be on standby so we could refuel a returning B-52 if there was an emergency that required it to have more flying time. After the flights returned that day at about noon, my crew had the afternoon off and went to the beach for some sun and beer.

A few days later, we escorted an EB-66 from Guam to the coast of Vietnam as it was on its way to Takhli.

My crew could either land in the Philippines and refuel our KC-135, or return to Guam if we felt we had enough fuel to make the trip. We determined that we had enough fuel for the return, but we had trouble getting flight clearance back to Guam. No one on the radio could understand us. They didn't speak English, and we didn't speak Chamorro. Since we couldn't get clearance, we had to climb to 41,000 feet to ensure we would not interact with any other aircraft. The last flight control airspace is at 39,000 feet.

We might have been making our way back to a tropical island, but at 41,000 feet, it felt more like the North Pole. The temperature fell to negative 40 degrees Celsius, and we could not heat the aircraft. Thankfully, we always carried our arctic gear with us. The boom operator opened our bags and distributed the parkas and mittens.

The thin air allowed the wiring to leak voltage, which in turn caused the instruments to go crazy. After three hours, we were finally able to contact the Guam approach. We became under their control and began our descent, but at about 25,000 feet, I thought it sure was foggy outside Guam. It didn't take long to realize that it wasn't a bad fog, but my window was frosted up because my window heater had become inoperative. Fuel was tight, and we had to land. I told my co-pilot he would have to do it because I couldn't see, and we didn't have time for the window to defrost in the warmer air.

He landed without any problems, and as we slowed, I opened my window to taxi the aircraft to its parking place. By that time, I figured that the Air Force knew what it was doing when it limited us to 120 hours of flying time per month. I was beginning to be slow to react because I was fatigued.

B-52S GO NORTH

In April of that year, the higher-ups at Strategic Air Command decided to send in B-52s to bomb North Vietnam for the first time. It was a big deal.

There were 30 tankers and 30 B-52 bombers assembled in Guam for this operation. While in Guam, tanker crews were given leftover quarters and poor service. It was a three hots and a cot situation.

Since the commander was still sour that I came into the squadron as a pilot and jumped ahead of his favorite guys to become AC, I was considered a nobody. For that great honor, I was assigned the number two flying position for this mission. Number two is the worst position because, being stuck in the middle, there is no wiggle room for error.

When the time came, my crew was number two on about the fifth group of threes to go for take-offs — a flight of three bombers would take off at one-minute intervals, followed by three tankers at one-minute intervals. Take off was made to the east over a 600-foot cliff. This went on for one hour as 30 B-52s and 30 tankers took off. My crew was right in the middle of this operation.

Three hours after all 60 aircraft became airborne, we assumed refueling positions. When the offload was finished, tankers turned toward Kadena, and the B-52s flew to North Vietnam, where they would drop 585 tons of bombs on the Mu Gia Pass near an entrance to the Ho Chi Minh Trail — the supply line for the North Vietnamese that ran through the mountains and jungles.

The next night, we resumed normal operations while everyone talked about the big deal bombing from the day before, but all the tanker guys knew they had just bombed a bunch of trees. We had been there before. The attack made big headlines, but by the next day, it was business as usual for the North Vietnamese on the Ho Chi Minh Trail. Any damage the B-52s caused was quickly repaired, and we had barely disrupted them.

U-TAPAO

We had just landed from a B-52 refueling mission when I learned that my crew and another crew would be flying a special air-refueling mission in the Gulf of Tonkin the next day and landing at U-Tapao Royal Thai Navy Airfield. Our mission to refuel a flight of eight F-4s would have to be completed before dark, because the airbase at U-Tapao was still under construction and the runway didn't have lights yet.

We were set to be picked up at 11 p.m., but at 10:45 p.m., a messenger informed me that there would be a four-hour delay. The new pick-up time would be 3 a.m. At 3 a.m., a bus arrived and took us to get our combat survival gear and codes for the mission. After the pre-flight check, we had an hour left before take-off. While we were waiting, we learned that the flight would be delayed for another four hours.

Finally, at 7 a.m., we departed Okinawa and headed for the Gulf of Tonkin. When we arrived, we learned that the F-4s would not arrive for four more hours. We remained airborne as we waited for them, and by the time they arrived, we had to notify headquarters that we did not have enough fuel to offload the amount that was scheduled. We were instructed to give all that we could and then make a landing at Da Nang Air Base in Vietnam. After we gave the F-4s enough fuel to complete their mission, we had 6,000 lbs. of fuel left, which gave us 45 minutes to land.

Upon approach to Da Nang, the air controller cautioned us that small arms fire was possible on the approach, but we were able to land safely. We took on 4,000 gallons of fuel and needed to leave Da Nang because time was running short if we wanted to land at U-Tapao before dark. The Da Nang airport did not have an air cart to start the engines, but we had an emergency cartridge that we could use to start one engine, and then use it to start the other three one at a time.

This method worked for my aircraft, but not for the number two aircraft, whose third engine would not start. I thought about the system for a minute and sent my crew chief over to coordinate with the #2 crew chief. I had them open the cowling and beat on the air control valve to the starter. The trick worked, my crew chief made his way back to our plane, and we headed for U-Tapao at dusk. We were headed west as the sun goes, and were able to land just before dark.

That was one long mission, and we were glad for it to end. The entire crew slept for 14 hours that night.

A few days later, we left U-Tapao for another refueling mission with fighter aircraft in the Gulf of Tonkin. After we offloaded the fuel, we turned left and began to climb to 41,000 feet. As my crew exited, we talked to Panama Control, and they advised us that there were no more aircraft ahead of us. We began climbing. I was getting comfortable and just as I removed my parachute, I looked out a small window above my head to see the tail end of another KC-135 staring me in the face. I quickly had to retard the throttles to idle and told the co-pilot that I had control of the aircraft. By this time, we were nearly under the other aircraft. I was afraid to pull the spoilers, because sometimes that raises you up. Finally, we began to separate. The other pilot never even knew we were there.

That could have been a fatal disaster for all of us, but by the grace of God, because before take-off, I had tried to close that little curtain above my windshield that covered the window where I looked out and saw the other plane. I couldn't get the cover to stay down. It seemed like a minuscule malfunction at the time, but it saved all of our lives.

After that close call, we were headed to a recovery point that was about 40 miles north of the airport at U-Tapao. Our radar became inoperative, and there was a huge wall of clouds ahead. I was not going into that storm without radars, so I climbed to 41,000 feet over Laos to the top of the clouds. I rolled the aircraft 90 degrees to the left and looked straight down at 40,000 feet of straight-edge clouds. As I rolled left and began the descent, it felt like I was weightless and falling off an eight-mile cliff. Everything turned out perfectly, but that feeling of falling will live with me the rest of my life.

MAY 1, 1966: MAYDAY

Our mission on April 30 began as any other. We had take-off at 3 a.m., did our refueling, and everything went routinely for the 21 tankers that had gone out that morning. However, when it was time to recover at the air base, things took a turn.

During a normal recovery, 21 aircraft can land in less than one hour. But monsoon season was upon us, and on this morning, there was a massive downpour of rain and winds that I'd only imagined happened during hurricanes. Kadena lost all its radar that morning, and that forced us to control our landings using a different procedure. Without the help of radar, we would have to control our landing intervals by time.

My aircraft was number 20 in line to land, which meant I would have to circle quite a while before I could begin to descend. The guy above me knew his fuel wouldn't last, so he went ahead to a different air base for his landing. If worse came to worst, I could have landed my KC-135 on the taxiway, but I wasn't going to let it get that far.

There I was, 30,000 feet above Kadena, looking down at 19 other aircraft below me. It was quite a task for all of us to maintain 1,000 feet of distance between us while we figured out how to get everyone on the ground.

After my first three approaches, it became obvious that I would run out of fuel if we followed the procedures that were in place, which required seven minutes for each plane's approach, and it was bad enough having to land downwind with a monsoon raging outside in an aircraft that didn't even have windshield wipers.

The way we were doing it, each aircraft was responsible for letting everyone else know when they reached 18 miles from the runway. When that happened, the next aircraft in line could begin descending, and so on. But if everyone was going to have enough fuel to remain airborne, there would have to be some shortcuts taken.

I radioed everyone and suggested that, in order to speed things up, we start calling it at six miles instead of 18, because nobody was moving and things were not looking good. It was simply taking too much time. Everyone agreed, and we began to step down 1,000 feet every time the leading aircraft reached the six-mile mark from the runway.

It looked like this was going to work, but not running out of fuel wasn't my crew's only concern during that landing.

KC-135s had 11 fuel tanks— four in the main wing, two in the wing tips, one in the forward body, one in the center wing, and one in the tail. It was originally a Boeing 707 that had been built as an airliner, and they didn't account for offsetting the weight of the boom we had to install for refueling purposes. So, to offset the weight of the heavy boom in the back, we always kept fuel in the forward body tank. But, we had used all the fuel that day, and that had the potential to make landing a real fiasco.

We knew our center of gravity was way in the back, so upon landing, the navigator and the boom operator would have to come to the front of the aircraft and hold on to the pilot and co-pilot seats. If we didn't balance the weight, the tail could hit the runway.

As we got set to land, the tailwind was wailing at 40 knots, which was about as bad as it could be. Our visibility was less than half a mile, so as we started to descend at the eight-mile mark, I opened the side window a few inches so I could see the landing. Windshield wipers sure would have come in handy. It seemed we were always being reminded of how low our bid for the aircraft was.

We ended up landing better than anyone, but the nose was bouncing up and down while taxiing in. The crew chief placed a pole under the tail to keep it from tipping before we left the aircraft. It was a relief to land safely. When all was said and done, we had finished the mission with only

125 gallons of fuel left. In other words, if we had been in the air for seven more minutes, we would have crashed. That's why we always referred to it as "Mayday"!

That wouldn't be the only time a tanker found itself in trouble due to monsoon weather at Kadena. Just a few weeks later, a buddy of mine crashed a KC-135 just after take-off. At Kadena, there were a lot of airliners coming in and out bringing injured or casualties, but on that day, the weather was so bad that even they weren't flying. Torrential downpours and strong winds made much of anything concerning flying impossible. But Yokota Air Base needed a spare jet engine.

A classmate of mine who had lived right down the street from us back in Albany, and his crew, were told to fly the mission, despite the bad conditions. He was a brand-new aircraft commander. He'd come from flying fighters and didn't have much experience flying the big birds. About the time he was taking off, controllers told him to abort the mission, but it was too late to stop. The crew lost control of the aircraft and crashed into a hill. The crash killed all 11 men onboard the tanker, and one civilian whose car was hit with debris.

It was a very solemn day at Kadena Air Base, a day that reminded us that bad things happen. It might have happened to me, and flying tankers was all I'd ever known. It could have happened to anybody.

I still stay in touch with his kids, and even recently had dinner with his daughter as she and her family were passing through Alabama on their way north.

COMING HOME

After six months in Southeast Asia, it was time for my unit to return to the States. Though we had a few close calls, my deployment had been interesting overall.

We were given a slot once a month to call our families, and of course, we could write a letter here and there. Other than that, there hadn't been much communication. The thought of being back home was wonderful.

While many service members who were deployed during the Vietnam War did not get a warm welcome back home, that was not the case for us. We flew back to Turner Air Field and were met by the happy faces of our eager families in the hangar. Lil and the girls were there. It's funny how much the children had grown and changed in just six months. It was good to see everybody and good to be back home.

Shortly after I got home, Lil and I had the opportunity to travel to New York City. Since I always try to find the cheapest way to do things, I sent Lil on an airliner and I flew out on an Air Force plane from Warner Robbins for free. I was supposed to meet Lil there, but the weather turned, and I had to land in Washington, D.C. I caught a train from there to NYC. Every airplane from Europe coming to New York had landed in D.C., and the train was packed with people from every nationality in the world. Boxes and bags of clothes were covering so much of the train that you couldn't even walk up and down the aisle. It was mayhem.

I finally got to the city around 3 a.m. Lil had long ago checked into the hotel, and she met me at the door, mad as hell, wondering where I had been all that time. Since there were no cell phones back in those days, it would have been difficult for me to contact her and let her know what had happened. I guess in some ways the spoiled trip could have been a sign of things to come.

THE END OF MY MARRIAGE AND THE CLOSING OF TURNER AIR FORCE BASE: 1967

In 1967, I was promoted to major, and I was finally assigned to the instructor upgrade program. That meant I could teach up-and-coming pilots how to fly. It was eventually announced that Turner Air Force Base would close. My wing was reassigned to McCoy Air Force Base in Orlando, Florida, but I did not go with them. Even though I'd been with them a while, they never got over me jumping ahead of the favorite boys for the pilot position. I was still nothing more than the bastard AC to them, and I was glad to be going in a different direction.

It was around this same time that Lil and I decided to call it quits on our marriage. We'd given it a good shot for two kids who had found themselves in the family way in the middle of college, but the pilot and the beauty queen just couldn't make it work.

I was assigned to Robins Air Force Base, and she stayed an hour and a half away from me in Albany with Sharon and Dawn (Sue was still living in Augusta). I traded in my 1957 Chevrolet for a top-of-the-line 1964 Chevrolet Corvair. It might have had all the bells and whistles of a nice car, but hell, it was still just a Corvair. At any rate, it held all my belongings, and it made for a smooth ride into bachelorhood.

I lived for a dollar a day at the BOQ at Warner-Robbins for as long as I could. For someone who likes to squeeze a dollar, there was no way to beat that low cost of living. Eventually, I was able to find a new furnished apartment that was secluded in the woods at the end of a road only a short distance from base. I liked it there because I had a lot more privacy than when I'd lived in the Bachelor Officer Quarters.

The complex had six apartments, and each had its own sitting area, kitchen, bedroom, a large bathroom, and an enclosed deck. My new apartment was also furnished with nice furniture and kitchen utensils. That was nice, since I had left everything like that with Lil and the kids. However, the apartment did not have a dishwasher. Lil, let me buy the dishwasher she'd won in the pageant from her. I didn't mind the expense, because I always liked clean dishes and cookware.

Lil and I were cordial for the sake of the children, but it was time to let the good times roll as far as I was concerned. Warner Robbins was heaven for somebody who had just gotten divorced. There were single women everywhere. Wining and dining all the good-looking women in town was fun, but it could cost a man a lot of money if he wasn't careful. I knew how to make a dollar stretch, though, and many of my dates were treated to buy one, get one free meals at local restaurants. If anyone ever called me cheap, I can't recall.

BACK TO VIETNAM

I never had another traditional deployment to support the Vietnam War effort, but I did make several trips back over, just filling in for a pilot or co-pilot who needed leave.

Still reeling in my newfound freedom, I found that these flights back overseas gave me the chance to date new and interesting women. On one occasion, I spotted a beautiful woman at the hotel bar. I was set to fly out of Bangkok the next morning, but I figured there was enough time before bedtime for a date.

I introduced myself to her and learned that she was from Germany. I asked her which room she was staying in, and she told me, but when I tried to call her room later, she wasn't there. I must have thought she was really beautiful, because I went through the trouble of calling the German Embassy to locate her. Turns out she was staying at a different hotel, but in the room number she had given. We enjoyed a lovely two-dollar steak that evening and became quick friends. I learned that she was well educated, with several college degrees. Perhaps the most interesting thing about her was that her father had been a part of a failed plot to assassinate Hitler. We stayed in contact for a while, and she invited me to stay at her chalet in Switzerland, but I never made it. There were too many other single women in the world to go through all that trouble for one date.

I flew my last missions for the war effort in 1968. One day, my crew was flying in support of an F-4 that was set to cruise over the Ho Chi Minh Trail on a reconnaissance mission to record what the enemy was moving during the night and early morning.

We were anchored in an area in the corner of Thailand, Cambodia, and Vietnam on a Saturday night when the F-4 called for fuel. Boy, it was dark. At that time, we depended on ground radar to connect us with the aircraft that needed refueling. Ground control out of Phnom Penh was trying to execute the rendezvous, but after three attempts, our aircraft and the F-4 were not even close to each other, and the F-4 was getting low on fuel. I later joked that the real radio operator had gone out on the town and left the houseboy running the place. In other words, to set up a successful rendezvous, you've got to know what you're doing.

When it became clear that we would not locate each other using ground control, an emergency rendezvous was executed. I remembered a method we had used in the old prop days, before radar, and I told the F-4 to transmit his radio on the refueling channel. I had him hold the transmitter switch on for ten seconds, and by using this old procedure, I was able to locate his direction, and we proceeded towards each other.

In less than 10 minutes, the F-4 stated that he needed fuel as soon as possible, so I reduced the offset to turn in front of him. At about the 45-degree mark on the left, I made a 60-degree bank turn at 350 knots, slowing to 320. We rolled out in front of the F-4 less than a half mile and 1000 feet above. I descended to the F-4 to save him from climbing, since he was dangerously low on fuel by this time. In less than one minute, the F-4 was taking fuel just as his low fuel light came on.

It was lucky for the F-4 pilot that we were able to locate each other using the outdated technology of the UHF radio signal. Otherwise, he would have had to bail out over the Gulf of Thailand. He would have had a hell of a time with all of his gear on, but anyway, it was a save.

Of all my time spent supporting the war, I only ever landed in Vietnam the one time we had to land in Da Nang for refueling before heading to U-Tapao. As a member of the Air Force, I wasn't as in touch with the fighting as service members from other branches were. So, when my time with the Young Tiger missions ended, I didn't have many feelings about it. It had just been my job, and I did it.

LIFE AT WARNER ROBBINS

In 1969, I was promoted to be one of the three standardization KC-135A pilots in my squadron. The job was the same as that of combat crew members, but I was an evaluator for the rest of the pilots and crews. I was happy with the job because it decreased my alert time, but it did require me to be at work daily, Monday through Friday. My new job meant that I became an expert concerning the KC-135 aircraft and the regulations and procedures required of a pilot, co-pilot, and crew members.

I evaluated crews using examinations to make sure they were operating using proper emergency and FAA procedures. I quickly learned how to develop exams that would successfully evaluate each person's knowledge. There was no finagling around the correct answer with me. If they failed, they would require more training. But that's how I made sure all of the pilots and crew members who went through me were skilled enough to perform their duties.

By this time, I had dated about a hundred women all over the world. Georgia, Alabama, Europe, Hawaii, Thailand, you name it. But my job responsibilities increased, and my time for playing the field decreased. My dating time became less and less. That meant I had to decrease the number of women I took out.

Lil remarried about nine months after our divorce was finalized. A rich man who lived on the lake. But I had taken time to re-sow my wild oats and enjoyed every minute of it.

My daughter Dawn.

My daughter Sharon.

Eventually, all good things come to an end. And sometimes a good thing ending can mean an even better thing begins. One day, I saw a lady I knew coming out of the liquor store. She had a friend with her — Patricia Hume— and she caught my eye. We began dating, and I guess we hit it off because before long, she was the only one I was taking out for two-for-one dinners.

Patricia was divorced, like me. Her husband had been sorry. She had two children, and she worked as an accountant at a bank. Eventually, my time as a bachelor ran out. I was tired of trying to keep up with so many women from here and all over. I knew it was time for me to settle down again, and as luck would have it, I fell in love with Patricia. We dated for around six months before we got married.

We had a small ceremony on April 1, 1970, at a little church with a reception at the Officer's Club afterwards. When the reception ended, Pat and I drove to Charleston Air Force Base, where we boarded a C-141 embassy flight to Rio de Janeiro, Brazil.

After about 10 hours in flight, we arrived in Brasilia, the capital of Brazil, where we had to leave documents for the state department and refuel. Then we made our way to our honeymoon spot. We had reservations at an all-inclusive hotel on the beach for only $19 a day. We were disappointed to find that our accommodations were located next to a four-lane highway. In addition to that, I unfortunately came down with the flu. That put a damper on our honeymoon for a few days. The trip seemed to be hindered by bad luck at all turns, because when I was finally well enough to enjoy the free food and the beach, I realized I'd forgotten to pack shoes. My time on the beach was spent wearing the same black military dress shoes I'd worn on our wedding day. No one in Rio wore shoes larger than a size 12, so I was stuck in my size 14 dress shoes for the entire trip.

After five days, we decided to move to a cheaper hotel that was two blocks away from the beach. I was disappointed that our food wasn't included in this price, but the new location allowed us to explore the restaurants and different nationalities on the beach.

On the way back to Charleston, we landed in French Guiana to refuel, and thankfully, the rest of the trip was uneventful.

Back at Warner Robbins, it was time for me to move my belongings to Pat's house. That June, we were able to get housing on the golf course at Robins Air Force Base. The 17th green tee was in my backyard. My navigator and I went together and bought a golf cart, which we stored and recharged in my garage. It amused us that Uncle Sam paid to recharge our cart.

Since it was summertime, Sharon and Dawn were staying with me. That gave us all the time to get acclimated as a family. It was a busy place, with four kids, two dogs, and our work schedules. But that life only lasted for four months, because bigger changes were on the way.

A MOVE TO CALIFORNIA

Somehow, my performance as a standardization pilot was noticed further up the chain of command, and I was selected to interview for Combat Crew Training at Castle Air Force Base in California. Since my organization did not have funds to pay for the trip, they gave me a free week of leave, and I hitchhiked across the country. It had been a long time since I thumbed a ride, and I was happy hitching as a member of the Air Force is different than catching a ride from a stranger as a college student. Instead of stalking down dusty roads waiting for someone to pick me up, all I had to do was find someone who was flying west and hop on their aircraft. The guy who took materials to Oklahoma City from Warner Robbins had room on his plane, and that was the first leg of my journey. It took three days, a couple of flights, and a bus ride, but I finally made it to my interview with Castle's commanding general.

I ended up interviewing with a wing commander who was a one-star general. He must have liked me, because he recommended me for the job. I left Castle that midnight in a pick-up truck that traveled each night to input data in the only available computer the area airbases had to use to request parts that needed to be delivered to other air bases. I was lucky enough to meet the Beale Air Force Base truck and ride back to that base, where I was able to catch a plane back east at 7 a.m. the next morning. The entire trip took six and a half days.

While I felt optimistic about having a new opportunity, I was not enthusiastic about having to move to California. I had been a student at Castle in 1963 and remembered that the housing station was horrible because every two weeks, a new class of 200 students would arrive and another class of 200 would leave. That made it hard to find housing, because no one wanted to mess up their 2-week rent schedules. I knew I would figure something out, though.

When I got back home to Georgia, I had only 45 days to get our family ready for the move. The first thing I did was sell our cars, and I replaced them with a Pontiac sedan, because it had an exceptionally large trunk that would be beneficial during our move. I planned transport for our two dogs and arranged for them to be boarded for one month.

On the morning of September 15, I left for California with Pat, her two children, and Sharon (Dawn had decided to stay back in Georgia with Lil.) After a long drive, we made a pitstop in Denver, Colorado, for a visit with Pat's parents. I had liked my first set of in-laws, and I was happy to be able to say the same about Pat's family. Her dad was pretty good, and her mother was a good old country gal who had come from Ukraine. He was an executive with Gates Corporation, and he met her when she was working as a housekeeper at a hotel. We rested there and visited with them for a few days, and then spent three more days traveling to California.

When we finally made it to the Golden State, we found a two-bedroom apartment. It was as horrible as I had expected the lodging to be. It was furnished, but we had to use dog food cans to hold the beds up off the floor. We took trips on the weekends just to get away. After a short time, I discovered that one of the permanent party navigators was moving out of his house, and he rented it to us for a year. It was close to the base, and even though it only had three bedrooms, we made it work by having the girls share a room. Moving into a real house made the adjustment easier on everyone.

After living in the house for around a month, I noticed that the large tree in the backyard was an English walnut tree, and it was loaded with nuts. I was accustomed to the wild black walnut trees back home, which bore nuts with shells you had to break into with a hammer, but to find the tame English walnut tree right there in my backyard was a treat. They were easy to crack and delicious to eat. It was my favorite nut, and I thought I had died and gone to heaven.

When I reported to my new job as a flight instructor, they wanted me to work in simulators for six months. Since I had so much experience, I argued that I should be able to go straight to instructing. The higher-ups agreed, though I did sometimes instruct crews using simulators when I wanted to enhance their emergency procedures.

Crews required ten flights and a flight examination before they graduated to their assigned base. That meant I had to fly every third day. That's how it went until each crew had ten flights under their belts and were ready to be tested on their capabilities.

A HOME OF OUR OWN

After living in our rented home for a while, it began to feel too small, and I started looking for a change. I finally located a piece of property about five miles from base that looked promising. It had a creek and a drainage ditch that converted to a waterfall. It was completely covered in bushes and vines that were as high as the treetops, but I figured I could take care of that, so I bought the lot and planned to build a house there.

I set out to eliminate the vines and found an easy way to do it. One winter morning, the fog was very thick. I knew that burning was taboo in California, but I also knew the heavy fog would mask the smoke. I took a chance and set a fire to clear off my property. Before long, all the vines and bushes were gone, and the large trees came out of hiding. I located a local builder and contracted to have a house built on the lot, but the builder suggested that I needed to add two feet of elevation before the house could be built.

My frugal heart was happy to find that the city of Atwater was updating its underground utilities and had free dirt available. In my spare time, I rented a dump truck and raised the lot two feet without having to pay for dirt or labor. I was thankful that I listened to the contractor, because two years later, a flood came and water got within nine inches of the house.

I was able to find other supplies for free along the way. One time, when I was making a trip back to Georgia to see Sue and Dawn, I noticed the golf course had a big pile of discarded sod because they had just redone the greens. I loaded them up and took them all the way back to California. Before long, I had the most beautiful yard you'd ever seen. Another time, I saw a pile of old culverts and located the owner, who agreed to let me take them off his hands. I was able to fix the drainage ditch at my house for free.

When everything was finished, I had a beautiful place. My family enjoyed having more space, and the dogs loved to play in the creek. It was always peaceful to look out in the yard to see quail and pheasant dusting under the trees.

We lived in our country home for about two years before one of my colonel friends told me that I would be getting an assignment to Strategic Air Command headquarters in Nebraska. I hated to leave the house we had built, but the commute from California to the Great Plains would have been too far. I listed the house, and someone instantly bought it. I made a good profit, and my family moved into a new three-bedroom house on base while we waited for my transfer. But it never came. I later found out that after visiting my house, my friend became jealous of where I lived and made up the story about my transfer. It was a pretty lousy joke to play on someone, but I got over it. He'd always been a butthole anyway, and I never cared for him.

ON THE GROUND

I'd been in the air since 1956, and I'd had my fill. With only a few years left to serve in the Air Force, I was ready for a change of pace, and I left the pilot seat and moved to academics, where I was a KC-135 Systems and Tactical Doctrines Instructor.

Teaching is considered one of the lowest jobs you can get in the Air Force, but as far as I was concerned, it was a decent 8-5 job. I still had to fly twice a month to maintain my combat-ready status, but other than that, I spent the rest of my career on the ground.

1974 was a big year for me. My hard work as an instructor paid off, and I was appointed Deputy Squadron Commander and Director of Academic Training of the 4017th Combat Crew Training Squadron.

I also earned my promotion to Lt. Colonel. It was really an honor. I was one of three people to receive the promotion that year out of 20 men who were eligible at Castle. I had known about the promotion early, because one of my friends in Washington, D.C., saw my name on the list prior to the official release of the names. Many of the "fair-haired boys" had not gotten promoted. That, paired with the fact that I was not a regular officer, but still a reserve, made my promotion surprising for a lot of people.

We had a huge promotion party at our house. It was a lot of work to spruce up our house, and we even bought new carpet. The place was rolling. A general even showed up. It was such a party that I had to call the liquor store and have more booze delivered. We had a good time, but Pat and I were glad when it was over and we could relax.

Me in my office in California.

RESHAPING THE 4017TH

In 1975, I was named Squadron Commander of the Combat Crew Training Squadron. The commander before me had quit, and it was probably partly my fault for giving him hell because he didn't know what he was doing. In all fairness, I wasn't the only one who had been on his ass. One day, he just up and left. That's how I got to be head chief in a hurry. It was no easy task being in charge of nearly 2,000 people. Every time someone needed anything, it came through me, from getting bailed out of DUIs to congressional investigations over not paying child support.

Speaking of that, I was the subject of a few of those because Lil had a habit of writing to Congress to tell them that I had not paid her. It wasn't true. Luckily for me, a colonel I worked with had the same type of ex-wife. It got to be a running joke.

The 4017th had been something that no one wanted to touch with a ten-foot pole. They'd been operating it out of old barracks that didn't even have air conditioning, and I had to come in and reshape the entire thing. Under my command, a new school building was constructed. We had state-of-the-art classrooms with an audiovisual team that was so proficient, I had to stop loaning out their expertise to other departments. The higher-ups wouldn't approve money to buy classroom equipment that would hold up to so much traffic, so I had all of the old desks refurbished. The general and I loaded up a truck with all of the old stuff and drove it down to Sacramento to be fixed. The only glitch was that we didn't have any gas in the damn truck to go back and pick up the load. I bought the gas and never got reimbursed.

By the time I was finished with the 4017th, it was a well-oiled machine. People begged to be there because I found good instructors, made academics fun, and gave people recognition when they deserved it. I had a lot of good people volunteer to come out of the flying units to work there, which isn't easy to do because the flying game is where the gravy is.

We went from primitive to state-of-the-art in a very short time. That made me proud, but the end of my 20-year commitment to the Air Force was approaching. When the promotion list for colonel came out at the beginning of 1976 and my name was not on it, I decided it was time to plan for our move back to Alabama.

In February, my bomb wing received a request for someone to attend water survival training in Homestead, Florida. No one wanted to go, but I had a plan, so I volunteered. Instead of flying straight to Florida, Pat and I flew to Alabama.

While we were there, we selected the place where we would build our new home. We picked out the perfect spot on some property that my dad had given me a few years back when he began to downsize his farm. Our new home would have the lake in the front, the mountains in the back, and a two-acre pond to fish from. What else could you want?

After a day or two back in Sauty Bottom, Mom and Dad drove us down to Homestead, where I endured three days of hell in the Florida backwaters.

I was the oldest one out there among what were mostly first-class airmen who were 18 to 20 years old. It kind of put a pep in their step to see a 42-year-old there, and they thought if I could do it, they could. If you want to picture what the training was like, just imagine you're parasailing over the Gulf and someone cuts your line. We had to figure out how to land in the water, inflate our raft, and get rescued by a helicopter. Most of the time, I felt like someone was trying to drown me. It wasn't easy. At times, it was frightening, but overall, it wasn't a big deal to me. However, I don't think someone pulled off the streets could have survived it. Anyway, I was glad to have the free trip back home.

A few months later, it was time for my career with the Air Force to come to an end. It had been a great career, a great life. I had a good experience and met a lot of good people. I wasn't sad because my goal had always been to leave at that time. The only thing that could have stopped me was a promotion to colonel, but even that wouldn't have kept me much longer. I wanted to go back home and try something new.

Before I left, my squadron threw me a wonderful retirement party. It was fantastic. The Officer's Club was completely full, which surprised me and made me feel like people had really appreciated my contributions and liked me there. I was also surprised when they presented me with the Distinguished Flying Cross, which is awarded for heroism and extraordinary achievement while participating in aerial flight. I wasn't aware that my navigator had nominated me for this honor due to the way I handled the situation back in 1968 with the R-4, which badly needed refueling and couldn't locate us coming out of Vietnam. I didn't really know what it meant at the time, but in hindsight, it was a great honor and a wonderful note to end my Air Force career on.

BACK TO MY ROOTS

In May of 1976, Pat and I sold our cars and packed up all of our California belongings. The family loaded up in our 27-foot motor home and headed east. The first night we stopped was 10,000 feet above Yosemite National Park. When we left our home, it was a hundred degrees and hot as blazes, but high up in the mountains that night, the mercury in the thermometer barely registered 22. The next night, we meant to camp in Death Valley, but since the temperature was forecasted to be 122, we decided to drive on to Las Vegas. From there, we made a stop in Denver to stay with Pat's parents, just as we had done on our way to California six years ago.

After many hours on the road, it was good to see the Alabama state line and know that I was finally back home. It was wonderful to be back, but I couldn't help feeling somewhat like a stranger. I'd been gone for twenty years, after all.

We hired a contractor and he began working on our house in July. In the meantime, we lived in an apartment in Scottsboro.

I purchased a 1956 Thunderbird to be our family wheels. A 1960 Corvair would be my personal running-around vehicle. It burned and leaked oil so badly that I became known as the mosquito man. I left a heavy trail of smoke everywhere I went. Luckily, it was only six miles from our apartment to the site of our future house.

Our new house will be located in close proximity to where I grew up. Back home meant back to the farm. I didn't consider myself a farmer anymore, though. The days of studying agriculture had been long forgotten. Still, I found myself helping Dad again. He gave me a few head of cattle to raise on my 40 acres. Otherwise, there wasn't as much to do because by this time, the only thing he was farming was hay. Good God, the old man sure did love his alfalfa. It just kept growing and growing, and we had to cut it about four times a year.

The haying work got to be more than I wanted to do, so I hired some high school kids to help us. One year, we had over 4,000 bales of alfalfa hay. The barns were bursting at the seams with it, and we had a stack out in the field as big as a building. Dad sold every one of them, and I didn't get a penny. That was okay, though.

Helping dad with the hay might have been a considerable amount of work, but it wasn't enough to keep me completely busy. It's a funny thing to be able to retire at the age of 43. I was still a young man. I guess I could have lived off my Air Force retirement, but I could not have lived as well as I wanted to. I still had the entrepreneurial spirit inside of me, and I'd been working on my MBA. I had ten courses left to take when we got back to Alabama, and going to school kept me occupied.

Our house was finished two days before Thanksgiving that year. The movers didn't bring the furniture until the next week, though, so we enjoyed one of Mom's home-cooked meals for Thanksgiving dinner.

Moving day came after a few days of rain. The yard was so muddy that the movers used the mattress covers to lay over the yard so our furniture wouldn't get ruined. After six months, it was nice to see all of our belongings again and begin to get settled.

In December came hog killing time. I hadn't seen a hog killed in close to thirty years. As the work began, I thought to myself, "A Lt. Col. isn't supposed to be killing hogs." But I did it for my dad.

He had five hogs to kill that year, and it was a big job. We started by killing the hogs with a 22 rifle. Then we had to put each one in a large tub of boiling hot water because scalding them would make it easier to scrape off the dirt and hair. After they were scalded, Dad hoisted them up using a front-end loader. He attached them to an A-frame rack by their feet. From there, their blood was drained, and he disemboweled them.

The weather was below freezing, so we had plenty of time as Dad took the hogs down and put them on an old table where he separated the legs, the head, shoulders, and the hind quarters from the carcass. We separated out the parts, lean from fatty. Nothing was wasted. Mom cooked the fatty parts, which were called rendering the fat for lard. She stored all that lard in five-gallon containers, and forty years after that hog killing, I found one of the old containers in the well house, and it was still full of lard. Mom combined the lean parts with the ears and nostrils to make souse meat — also known as head cheese.

Dad broke the carcass down. He cut hams, shoulders, middles, and necks. When all the hard parts were done, we put all the meat up in my motor home to cure for five days (of course, we covered everything in the motor home so it wouldn't be ruined). After that, we processed everything into ham, bacon, and sausage. When all was said and done, we had so damn much meat. We dispersed it here and there, and I guess it eventually all got eaten.

I was happy that Dad seemed to have had enough of hog killing after that. He didn't raise any more hogs, and when the meat ran out, he just went to the grocery store for more, like most everybody else was doing by then.

WEE PUTT AND OTHER ENDEAVORS: 1977

About this time, FedEx began hiring pilots, and I submitted an application to the employment office. I wasn't hired, and so I continued with my college courses and tended to my cattle.

In April, the opportunity arose for me to buy a miniature golf course in Scottsboro. I'd been busy with my business courses, and I figured I could at least try the business on for size. I borrowed $22,000 from the bank at 20% interest to make the purchase, and as quickly as I collected my first $5,000, I paid it on the loan. Every day, I'd open up shop at 5 p.m. and stay open until everyone was finished with their putt-putt game.

By the end of summer, I could see plain as day that this business was not for me. I didn't like working while other people were playing. I tried to sell it, but no one wanted it. Finally, I got the idea to add a batting cage. I figured someone could make enough money with that and the miniature golf together to provide for a family. Plus, I was ready to hand over the high interest rate to a new owner. I was finished with it. I found a buyer and washed my hands of it.

I couldn't keep the desire to fly from creeping into my soul, but I couldn't afford the cost at the time. I did some research and figured out that I had some funds left on my GI Bill. With that, I was able to get certified as a flight instrument instructor. That meant I would be able to teach others to fly using only their aircraft's instruments. This was something I'd done my entire military career, but most people flying small aircraft depend on sight to fly. It was a piece of cake to get the certification, because I could fly better than my instructor.

This got me back in the air on Uncle Sam's dime again for a short time, but it wasn't the money maker I'd hoped it would be in the long run.

Nevertheless, it got me back in the cockpit, and before long, the owner of a trucking corporation hired me to be his personal pilot.

I got to know him because he had a twin-engine Piper Comanche parked at the airport where I took my lessons to become a certified flight instructor. I asked my instructor if I could fly it, and he said, "If you can start it, you can fly it."

I talked it over with the owner, and he told me to take off and make three landings with it. I hopped in, looking forward to a solo flight, and just as the cabin door was shutting, he hollered, "The landing gear light may be on when you lower the gear. Just turn the master switch on and off, and it will go away."

Upon hearing this, I started the plane, but the throttles were set too high and the propellers were running too fast. Just imagine that you've just started your car with the accelerator pressed halfway down. The force was so much that I blew a piece of sheet metal off the hangar.

It didn't keep me from taking off, though, and I decided to head to the Huntsville airport for landing. Sure enough, when I lowered the landing gear, the red light he had warned me about came on. That red light meant it was not safe for landing, but I flipped the switch off and back on, and the light went out like he said it would.

I charged him $100 a day plus expenses. We mostly flew to Panama City, Florida, and Lubbock, Texas. I logged about 200 hours in the Comanche before he upgraded to a larger twin-engine Cessna 405. It was pressurized, and that meant we could fly above 12,000 feet and up to 17,000 feet. On long flights, it was safer between those altitudes, because smaller aircraft are below and larger airliners are above.

I will never forget the time I was bringing his children down to Panama City and one looked out the window at all of the clouds and asked, "Do you think we'll see Jesus?" I always thought that was priceless.

There are a lot of stories I could tell from this job. The business owner was the grouchiest, dirtiest, crudest person I've ever seen. I didn't care for him much, but I liked making money, and I liked being in the air.

One day, we were supposed to leave for Lubbock at 9 a.m. He was a big guy with a big belly, and he was scheduled to get a gastric band in Houston. He didn't show up until late in the day, and it was 7 p.m. before we made it to Texas. The next morning, he told me he needed me to pick somebody up in Kansas. So I did, and then flew back to Alabama. When I went to put the plane in the hangar, it was locked. He had changed the locks! I guess that was his way of firing me. He ended up hiring a kid to fly him for half of what I was charging. Good riddance. I was glad to get away from him anyway.

AUTOMOBILE CONSUMER SERVICES CORPORATION 1978

After Pat and I were settled in our new home, I decided it was time to let go of the motor coach. I sold it for $5,000, and the new owners were none the wiser that I had recently used it to cool down a year's worth of freshly slaughtered hogs.

I'd offloaded the putt-putt business and finished my MBA. I was getting antsy after being so rudely let go without so much as a "thank you for your time" or "kiss my ass" from my piloting gig. I'm not one to let my hands get idle, and that extra cash from selling the motorhome was burning a hole in my pocket. It was about that time James Killian, an old friend from high school, reached out to me.

Killian owned a little mom-and-pop store in Scottsboro. He sold a little bit of everything and a lot of nothing there, but he was a pretty good businessman, and he knew someone who had an opportunity he thought I might be interested in. He put me in touch with a man named John Bates, who said he had a business idea but didn't know how to make it successful.

Bates was a military man, like me. He had been a warrant officer during his career, and met a guy in Florida who had a business selling extended warranties for cars. When he retired from the Army, Bates decided he would start his own warranty business, but seeing as how he had spent years in the military and outside of that, he'd only ever worked as an usher at a movie theater, he didn't know how to get the ball rolling.

The first time I met John, he was sitting in his office, if you could even call it that. It was located in Room 1 at a dilapidated and closed-down motel located off the South Parkway in Huntsville. There, my soon-to-be business partner was, sitting at an old card table with his typewriter. I would come to find out that John was a hell of a guy, and an excellent typist who could whip up 120 words in a minute. He didn't know much about business, though.

That's where I came in with my MBA and the entrepreneurial blood that had been flowing through my veins since back in the days when I'd gather eggs to trade the rolling store man for a pack of Juicy Fruit. Besides, I thought the business was a good idea. Back then, you might get a short warranty on your car, but not the six-year, 100,000-mile warranty you get when you buy a new car today. It was a service of protection that people would want.

I invested my $5,000, and that bought me 5,000 shares in his company — Automobile Consumer Services Corporation. I thought this could be my greener pasture. It certainly sounded more up my alley than watching people play putt-putt on a Saturday night.

One of the first orders of business was to get us out of that motel room. I had a buddy who owned an insurance company on Bob Wallace Avenue in Huntsville, and we were able to set up an office inside his building. Incidentally, he sold me a cancer policy that I still have today.

I don't know if I could have imagined just how green this pasture was going to get over my lifetime, but it was something new to sink my teeth into.

John and I decided we would focus our sales calls on Tennessee and Alabama. For the next little while, he took the west, and I took the east. The two of us travelled to every car dealership we could find, peddling our extended auto warranties.

In the beginning, we simply had to make things up as we went. The first warranty we offered was $200 for three years or 36,000 miles.

I declared myself Vice President and CEO of the company, and the wheels of the future were set in motion.

MY LAST FLYING VENTURE:1982

Flying has always been one of the great loves of my life. Even though ACSC needed my full-time attention, I couldn't completely tear myself away from the sky. In the early 80s, a couple who owned a construction business approached me about going into business with them. We would purchase an aircraft together, I would fly it here and there for business ventures, and additionally, we would charter the plane. We thought those extra outside flights would bring in enough income to pay for the plane, its fuel, and any required maintenance.

I researched a list of airplanes for sale that would meet the requirements to carry five passengers and 1,000 pounds of cargo. It also had to cost less than $80,000. I finally happened across the perfect airplane— a Beechcraft Baron Model 58. Known as the "Cadillac of Twins," it was loaded with the latest technology.

We bought the plane, and since I had already flown the Cessna 405 for the trucking company, it was no trouble passing an FAA check ride and test to carry passengers. I picked the airplane up in Atlanta's smaller Northside airport and flew back to Alabama.

I flew the contractors everywhere they needed to go for business, and began the charter company, which I called Clemens Air Charter Service. I made flights as far north as Bridgeport, New Jersey, and as far south as Orlando, which was the location of one of my most memorable flights.

I had taken a few people from an accounting firm in Huntsville down that way, and as we were preparing to return home, it appeared that the weather would be too bad to conduct the flight. We tried to find a hotel in

Snow at the Yankton Airport.

Dad on our hunting trip to South Dakota.

Me with a few pheasants on our South Dakota hunting trip.

the area, but had no luck. We decided to fly ahead to Tallahassee and see what was going on there. We arrived, and it appeared that the weather was clearing up, so we decided to go ahead and finish the trip home that night.

We arrived at Huntsville International Airport around 2 a.m. The storm had calmed, and everything was still. Since there were no communications at that hour, it was the most silent landing I ever made. The bad weather made for heavy fog, and as I made my final approach, with no help from the control tower, I almost decided we wouldn't be able to make the landing. I couldn't see a thing. Then all of a sudden, the runway lights appeared straight ahead. I was able to make the landing, and it was a great feeling.

I guess the best flight I took was when I flew my dad and my old Air Force buddy on a pheasant hunting trip to Yankton, South Dakota. This was a trip Dad and I took every year, but having the opportunity to fly him there was a lot better than having to drive all that way.

We started our flight at 7 a.m. on a cold October morning from the airport in Scottsboro. Upon arrival at the airport, the Baron had been removed from its hangar. I performed a careful preflight inspection and paid special attention to the fuel tanks, since we were about to set out on a nearly five-hour flight and the fuel gauges weren't too accurate.

The takeoff temperature was about 30 degrees, but there was no frost on the wings. The heater on the aircraft could only be used in flight, so we couldn't check that before takeoff. I had used it with success on other trips, but I just couldn't seem to get it going during that flight. It didn't take us long in that weather to decide we needed to put on our warm hunting garb well before we faced the cold winds of South Dakota. It wasn't a warm flight, but I'd flown colder ones.

We decided to land in a little town an hour before our arrival in Yankton so we could warm up, use the bathroom, and refuel just in case we were running low.

When we finally made it to Yankton, the hunt went as planned for the most part. We walked the field rows for several days, flushing out a great deal of wild pheasant.

On the last day of our trip, there was a snowstorm that dropped 10 inches of snow on us, but luckily, when we arrived at the airport, the taxiway and the runway had been cleared. We loaded up our plane with our limit of pheasant, plus several more than our host had given us. The trip home was uneventful, except that it was still cold.

I was happy to have been able to fly my dad on that trip.

My business partners ended up having to declare bankruptcy, which put a halt to my flying for them. Luckily for me, the airplane we had purchased together was not included in their settlement. I decided to sell the Barron. I had no interest in making the monthly payment alone, and I was only breaking even at best with the charter business. I found a buyer and delivered it back to Atlanta.

My time in the clouds was over. At least at my time in the clouds as a pilot, anyway. 3264LIMA would be my last call letters.

It must have been bittersweet to fly an aircraft for the last time. I hardly remember it now. Being a pilot was my life for many years, but just like my time on the football field came to an end, so too did my time in the captain's chair.

I'd been a farm boy, an all-star athlete, and an airplane pilot.

Now, it was time to be a businessman.

ACSC GROWS

John and I were doing the best we could with ACSC, but for a while, we were only able to convince what felt like a handful of dealerships to buy our warranty. I told John, "This ain't going to hack it." There just wasn't enough money coming in. The bills of the company were being paid, but John and I were not making a dollar to bring home.

I'd recently chartered a local chapter of a club for retired military officers, and I belonged to the Military Officers Association of America. Every so often, they would send me a publication in the mail, and I wondered what would happen if we advertised our warranty business in their magazine.

I figured there was only one way to find out, so I made my way to Washington, D.C., for a meeting with MOAA to get the ball rolling. I was excited about the prospect of retired officers all over the nation seeing my business when they perused their periodical. But this brought about another challenge. Would a retired officer in New York City, or even Atlanta, make a long-distance phone call to Alabama about an extended auto warranty? Being pretty frugal myself, I figured the answer was probably not.

I called up AT&T to see how I could go about getting a toll-free number for ACSC. We were the first 1-800 number for a business in town — 1-800-824-7059. We still have the number today. It took them two months to come out and install it, but after that, the business really started booming, as they say.

It wasn't too long before we had to move to a larger office. It was still in the same building, but we could never get AT&T to come change our phone line over. Eventually, I had to crawl through the attic and do it myself. Later on, when we moved further down the road to yet a bigger office, it took AT&T forever to come out and move our line again. I sure wouldn't recommend them for speed. For the longest time, we had to leave a secretary at the old office to sit and answer phone calls. Finally, about six weeks later, they came and moved the line, and it was a good thing because the business was taking off.

John and I were the first on the block with this business, and we ended up being pioneers of the extended warranty. Our service gave people a sense of peace, because if their engine failed and they had our warranty, we would pay to have the engine replaced. We offered installment plans if they couldn't pay for the entire warranty up front, and we accepted credit cards.

In 1983, our company reached $200,000 in sales. That was decent money for back then, and it gave us the drive we needed to keep working hard.

FROM TYPEWRITERS TO COMPUTERS: 1984

In just a few short years, our company had gone from two guys making cold calls to a thriving business that was actually making money and had expanded its sales coverage nationwide. It takes a lot of work and organization to keep something like that growing successfully, so I guess it wasn't too surprising when we had some confusion with the state of Florida in 1984. They sent auditors to Huntsville to inspect us and ended up telling us we had to stop our sales there.

The simple gist of it was that we were not able to handle the computations required to figure out a five-year warranty under Florida's requirements, and that wouldn't cut it. At that time, we were still operating with filing cabinets and typewriters, but it became clear that we would have to upgrade our technology if we wanted to keep expanding.

A friend of one of my employees was able to help us set up a program called D-BASE. He showed up to our office dressed in mechanic coveralls and adapted the program for our business. I wouldn't have thought by looking at him that he was any sort of computer genius, but after he set us up, we could handle all of the computations required on our computers, and it was easier for us to keep records. I guess you could say we were moving into the digital world.

Throughout the 80s, the company continued to flourish. We even had the honor of receiving an award from Congress in Washington, D.C. for being the best small business in 1985.

In 1986, I hired our first claims manager, Jim Duffey. I sometimes called him "Crazy Jim." He was quite a character. He knew more jokes than Jack Benny, the dirtiest damn jokes you ever heard in your life. But if anybody had a problem, they called him. He could BS anything, and therefore could smell BS a mile away. He was a good mechanic, too, and all that came in handy when dealing with mechanics in charge of repairing vehicles that had filed a claim.

Jim was just one of the many employees our company would hire throughout the years. At its height, ACSC employed 36 people. Not too bad for a little startup that began conducting business at a card table in a rundown motel room.

JOHN BATES RETIRES: 1988

As the business got bigger, its inner workings became more complex. We hired staff to help with claims, collections, and computer analysis, and my business partner John began to feel that his time with ACSC was coming to an end. He was getting older, and I believe he felt he had accomplished his dream of establishing a vehicle warranty company. In 1988, he sold me his half of the company's stock, which was 15,000 shares. I managed to buy him out by paying him $50,000 up front and then paying him $2,000 per month, with no interest, until the deal was paid for.

I will always remember John as a wonderful and giving individual. He was gentle and never lost his cool. I joked that I wondered what it was like for such a person to have to be around me all that time.

John passed away in 2015 and was buried with military honors at Huntsville Memory Gardens. My wife and I continued to visit with his widow until the pandemic of 2020.

ACSC AND THE USDOT: 1990

I was describing my business to a friend of mine, and he mentioned to me that a meeting would soon be held in D.C. by the United States Department of Transportation to discuss importing vehicles. The Imported Vehicle Safety Compliance Act of 1988 had recently been signed and passed, and that meant vehicles that did not meet federal safety standards could no longer be imported into the United States. I'd met a lot of importers through my warranty business and even warrantied vehicles that were brought over from Europe and Asia. I had a feeling there was an opportunity to get a piece of that pie. I was right.

No stranger to the D.C. area, I made my way to the USDOT building. I wasn't sure I had the right credentials to be admitted to a federal building, but luckily, when I showed up, all I had to do was show them my military identification. I was granted admission to the building and made my way to the meeting that would end up making me my fortune. It was a great surprise to me that I was actually more familiar with the regulations needed to import a vehicle to the States than many of the other participants in the meeting, including the Department of Transportation personnel.

While I was in Washington, D.C, I visited an old friend. His name was Gene Methvin, but I called him Tiger. He had been a walk-on football player at the University of Georgia back when I played. He wasn't very good, and I think he made the team because the coach was courting his mom. But I was his mentor and tried to help him out. We stayed close friends, and I liked to stay with him and his wife when I visited their neck of the woods.

Like me, Tiger had become a pilot in the Air Force after we graduated from college, but he had a brilliant brain and left the service as soon as his compulsory service was over. He went on to become a well-known journalist. He wrote books and wrote for magazines and eventually became the senior editor of the Washington D.C. bureau of Reader's Digest.

Several years after this visit, Gene's wife was killed when a speeding car hit her as she was crossing the street.

He only lived a few years after that. I went to both of their funerals in Georgia, and still miss them today.

I enjoyed staying with Tiger and his wife, who happened to be a model. During our visits, we would drink and dine, and he would counsel me about my government contracts, because he knew a lot of important people in D.C. (he had even served on President Reagan's Commission on Organized Crime).

I was thankful for his hospitality and his advice. Shortly after the USDOT meeting in D.C., I signed an agreement with the DOT to underwrite a contract that each imported vehicle that entered the United States would conform to all of the safety regulations required by them and the United States Environmental Protection Agency. In other words, if a dealer wanted to import a vehicle from another country, he had to register with my company. We would certify that all of the correct modifications were made and keep up with this information for USDOT.

And, ka-ching.

Each time someone registered an imported vehicle through ACSC, they had to pay us a fee. With a good money exchange rate, many importers in Canada began buying in Canada and shipping vehicles to the United States. Needless to say, business for us along the Canadian border was booming, and I was well on my way to becoming prosperous.

That year, I purchased a large office building on Poole Drive in Huntsville so that Automobile Consumer Services Corporation could continue to expand. In 1991, we grew to multi-million dollar sales in Canada.

TRAVELS WITH PAT: 1991

My second marriage seemed to be going better than my first. I was very busy traveling the four corners of the country, running my business, and Pat mostly stayed back at our home in Sauty Bottom.

That must have gotten lonely for her at times, but when I wasn't dealing with business, we made time to travel together. One of our best trips was in the mid-eighties when we went to Newfoundland. I had always wanted to go there as a civilian since I had spent so much time there serving on alert when I was in the Air Force. When we got there, it had been many years since I'd seen it, and much had changed. Still, we enjoyed visiting the fishing villages and taking the ferry to Prince Edward Island and Nova Scotia while we were there. One of the most memorable parts of the trip was actually a trip to the grocery store that sold interesting foods from all over the world. An important lesson I learned was that the Canadian egg McMuffin from McDonald's is significantly different from the one served in the United States. Overall, it was a nice trip.

In 1991, we decided to take an even bigger and better trip.

Pat and I had become close friends with a couple named Hoyt and Pat Ferguson. I'd met Hoyt through the retired officers' club. We liked to play golf together when there was time for it, and the two Pats hit it off. We were all best friends, really.

For whatever reason, the four of us decided that we would like to visit Australia, and so we did.

Early one morning, we left the Huntsville Airport. We flew to Atlanta and then to Los Angeles. From there, we flew to Hawaii, and then we made the 12.5-hour flight to Cairns, Australia.

To say we were feeling fatigued when we landed might be an understatement, but they say you have to press on to avoid jet lag, so that's exactly what we did. We toured some large hills where coal had been mined, and then we visited the hillsides where they grew grapes for wine. We struggled through the day, made it to dinner, and then we crashed.

After a good night's rest, we went on a sailing expedition to the Great Barrier Reef. They were beautiful and breathtaking. It was a group tour, and we all had the opportunity to go diving for an up-close view of the reefs. Only I and a big, heavyset woman went. We kept bumping into each other underwater, but it was worth it to be able to see the reefs up close. I'd seen some in Thailand, but these were so much larger and more exquisite. The fish and flowers I saw were something that will be a lifetime remembrance.

The next morning, we boarded a flight for Alice Springs.

The town had a population of about 12,000, and its highway stretched for thirty miles. This was during Australia's spring, so the flowers were lovely and the palm trees made it feel like we were at the beach. But it was hot in the daytime. 125 degrees, but a dry heat. We observed several vineyards and learned about Alice Springs' first telegraph line.

That night we saw Crocodile Dundee in the theater, and found ourselves laughing after everyone else did because it took us longer to understand the Australian dialect and jokes.

After that, we took a train to Victoria. It had one bedroom, and we were happy to be able to rest after a long day of sightseeing. The train made several stops to pick up and deliver passengers at small one-room stations along the way. In the morning, the porter brought us an Aussie breakfast of tea, toast, and eggs. By this time, we were approaching Victoria, where we were set to explore more of Australia's beauty. Unfortunately, the Formula 1 race was in town and we could not find a reservation anywhere.

We settled on renting a car and exploring Victoria for only the day. It was a beautiful city, but since we couldn't stay, we later flew to Sydney. While we were there, of course, we enjoyed seeing the famous Sydney Opera House.

Hoyt and I heard about a local Rotary meeting, and since we were Rotarians back home, we decided to drop in on the Aussie Rotarians. They were so welcoming and asked us a lot of questions about the United States. They even let Hoyt and me win the raffle, and we were able to take two bottles of Australian wine home with us.

After a lovely time in Australia, the four of us flew to New Zealand. We arrived early in the morning and set off to visit the capital buildings and a glowworm cave. On the way to the cave, cars kept passing us and yelling "boot!" It took a while to realize they were trying to tell us that our trunk was open. Who knew they had a different name for it? We must have driven for a while with it flapping in the wind, but fortunately, we didn't lose any luggage.

After we visited the glow worm cave, we decided to visit a mineral salt spring. On the way there, we stopped at a shop and there were a lot of Japanese tourists visiting. Hoyt told them that I was an NFL player, and they gave me a good look-over because I was a giant compared to them.

When we arrived at our destination, there was a Japanese flag flying at the entrance. Hoyt had fought in World War II and hated Japanese people. It took all three of us to convince him to go in, but finally he did. We enjoyed the warmth of the springs, but never conquered the rotten egg smell of the sulfur water.

After that, we drove back to the capital and flew to Christchurch, New Zealand. One of the most interesting things was a museum about Antarctic history. We were able to see all of the equipment used there for the past 200 years.

We enjoyed visiting the Antarctic, and I noted that there were no birds there. The countryside was beautiful and very clean. One of the interesting side trips was through the mountain where we saw bridges built by

WWII Japanese prisoners to a coastal area on the far south side of the South Island — about 600 miles from the South Pole.

On the last night in NZ, we ate at a city-owned restaurant, and the manager let Hoyt and me make our own drinks. Our trip was almost over, and it had been a good one. We were scheduled to fly back to Australia and then fly to Hawaii and catch a ride back to the mainland, but Hoyt wanted to visit the American Air Base in New Zealand first. When we went there, we figured out that we could skip the flight back to Australia because they had a flight leaving for Hawaii that night. We made the arrangements, and the two Pats, naturally annoyed by the last-minute change of plans, hurried to pack up all of our stuff.

Hoyt could be a character, to say the least. He not only didn't care for Japanese folks, but he had a sore spot for women in charge, too. When he found out that the aircraft commander was a female, he said he refused to take the flight. Once again, the three of us had to talk him into it. The change of plans had been his idea, and it was too late to make any more changes. It was a great flight. The two Pats got regular seats, and Hoyt and I took side seats. That arrangement was okay with us, because after takeoff we could lie down and take a semi-comfortable nap.

We got to make a pitstop in Fiji, and then when we landed in Hawaii, the aircraft commander had already made us reservations at the BOQ, where we could stay overnight until our flight the next day.

It was a long flight back to California, and we stayed there a couple of days to help our bodies adjust to the time change. After 27 days of travel, the four of us landed back in Huntsville, Alabama. It was the trip of a lifetime, remarkable in every aspect. And one of the best parts was that we only spent $2,500 per couple.

MY MOTHER DIED IN 1991

My mother, Sue Lee Clemens, passed away on November 21, 1991. She'd been diagnosed with lung cancer not too long before she died. Mom had been a smoker at one time, but we weren't sure if that's what caused the cancer or not. It could have been hereditary, since she had a few sisters die from the same thing. She lived to be 82 years old. That was pretty good for those days.

She'd been a quiet woman, the type who would as soon jump under a kitchen table and hide as she would talk to someone who came in that she didn't know too well. But she was a good cook and a hard worker. I'll never forget how I clung to her in my early years as Dad was away working in the fields, how we'd gathered eggs together, and she'd fed me oatmeal every morning for breakfast. She was a good woman and a good mother.

The early 90s were a tremendously busy time for me. I was flying all over the nation handling my business affairs, and I guess that didn't lend much time for stopping by the little brick house on the corner where my parents lived. But it was so sad to say goodbye to Mom. We buried her at Pine Haven Memorial Gardens in Scottsboro.

Thanksgiving was a somber and lonely day that year.

Mom and Dad celebrating their 50th wedding anniversary.

CHRISTMAS IN HAWAII: 1991

I continued to advertise ACSC's auto warranties with the Military Officers Association of America, and as such, sometimes had to travel to their events. In December of 1991, they held a conference in Hawaii. Pat and I, along with Hoyt and his Pat, decided to take the trip together.

The meeting was held at a large hotel in Honolulu, and since I was a vendor, I had to set up an exhibit. When I went to set up, the manager approached me and told me that he needed my space and asked if I could wait to set up until the next day. He offered to set us up with a fancy dinner, and since I only needed an hour to set up anyway, I took him up on it.

That night, the four of us dined on the roof of one of the best restaurants in town. It was a wonderful dinner, and I was glad I had let the man use my space until the next day.

This was the end of December, and since my kids were with their mother and Pat's kids were with their father, we all decided to spend Christmas in Hawaii.

After my business with MOAA concluded, the four of us flew to the Big Island. Hoyt and I enjoyed a round or two of golf while we were there, but the highlight of the trip was having Christmas dinner under the palm trees while we enjoyed a nice ocean breeze. Mele Kalikimaka.

It was a wonderful trip.

THE END OF MY SECOND MARRIAGE: 1994

Pat and I were married for 24 years when I realized it was over. At least I can say that my second marriage outlasted my first. Pat had been different than Lil. I met her after a whirlwind of romances with women all over the world, and at a time when I was tired and wanted to settle down.

I guess you could say I was burnt out on the bachelor life and landed with Pat. She hadn't been a beauty queen, nor did she have the air of one, and I appreciated that in her. I liked to say, "She was a good ol' Yankee."

To tell you the truth, as I remember it, the straw that broke that camel's back was the fact that she wouldn't quit smoking. The damn house smelled like a nicotine den.

We had a lot of good years raising each other's kids together, but sometimes things just fizzle out. And that's what happened with us. I was so busy growing my business, and she was stuck in the country alone. Tale as old as time. We grew apart and went our separate ways.

Our divorce was finalized in 1995, and she is still on the payroll at ACSC. I'm fine with that.

MEETING ANNETTE: 1995

I met my current wife, Annette, shortly after Pat and I parted ways. She was the CEO of a large credit union in Huntsville, and our mutual friend, Faye, had tried to set us up on a date a time or two. I told Faye no, because I'd met her through my warranty business and thought she was ugly. But, as it turned out, I was thinking of the wrong person. The lady I didn't find attractive had died.

One weekend, Faye called me and said Annette was staying with her and they thought it would be nice if I took them out to dinner.

I had no other plans, so I took the ladies to dinner in Chattanooga at the Fifth Quarter. We had a nice time, and I always joke that it ended up being the most expensive dinner I've ever had.

My business was in Huntsville, and since that's where Annette worked, too, we began having lunch together frequently. After we got to know each other, we fell in love.

Annette and I dance at a Christmas Party. Meeting Annette 1995.

MEETINGS OF THE NATIONAL IMPORTER
AUTOMOBILE DEALERS ASSOCIATION

About every six months, the National Importer Automobile Association held a meeting. I wasn't obligated to go to these meetings, but it was a good way to sell my importing service.

The meetings were very useful to everyone involved because there were a lot of modifications that had to be made to vehicles before they could legally be driven in the United States, and the meetings helped keep everyone up to date and educated.

Over the years, I attended meetings in Toronto, Niagara Falls, Buffalo, Chicago, Kelowna, and Thunder Bay. The travel was good for business, but I also made a lot of good memories on these trips.

I always began my business trips in Nashville. It is much cheaper to fly from Nashville than from Huntsville, and I like to get a good deal. If I can, I will take advantage of the Bachelor Officer Quarters, because that is much cheaper than staying in a hotel. One way to make a dollar is to save a dollar, and the trips still usually turned out nice, even if we didn't make a point of staying in swanky hotels.

In 1995, Annette accompanied me on a trip to Kelowna for an important meeting. The weather was perfect on this trip, and the river there was softly flowing south. While we were there, we visited a winery. The grape harvest was complete, but there were grapes that remained on the vine. I learned that these were used for ice wine. For this, they would pick the grapes early in the morning while they were frozen and process them at the winery. I found the wine overpriced, but I sucked it up and bought the smallest bottle they had. I didn't think it tasted very good, but it was a novelty back in Alabama.

The next year, Annette and I traveled to the import meeting in Seattle. We travelled cheaply as always, which Annette didn't seem to mind. On this particular trip, she was suffering a migraine headache. After the long flight from Nashville, we stayed overnight at a BOQ, and the next day we had to take a ferry. That didn't help her migraine, so the next day she had to stay in bed. Since she felt a bit better the next day, we took a ferry to Victoria, Canada, because we wanted to do some sightseeing. It was much colder than we had expected, and we nearly froze to death. Luckily, we were able to purchase sweatshirts from a gift shop when we arrived. It was a nice trip, although I wondered if Annette would ever travel with me again since it took her two days to recover after she got back home.

Another year, I took my daughter, Dawn, and my granddaughter, Jenna, along to the meeting, which was held in Watertown, New York. Once again, we flew from Nashville, and to this day, those girls joke that I got them the cheapest seats on the plane just because they got stuck in the very back where they couldn't recline.

Nevertheless, I think it was a nice trip.

We lodged in Alexandria Bay in a spacious lodge. The next day, we chartered a boat and took a ride down the Saint Lawrence River, where we had a mediocre tasting dinner together and visited the Naval museum. One of the most interesting parts of the trip was getting to see Franklin Roosevelt's yacht. It was a funny-looking thing, and we got to drive it out on the Saint Lawrence Seaway about 100 yards. I thought it was funny because about a decade earlier, I had visited FDR's home place at Hyde Park with my ex-wife Pat at the end of our Newfoundland trip. My dad always hated him as a president because of his farm policies, but there I was visiting his house and riding his yacht. I don't think Dad would have been impressed with it.

Perhaps one of my biggest memories of my trips to the importer meetings was the time I caught a ride with a man who did some of the paperwork for my company.

I always try to make a dollar go a long way, of course, so instead of flying to Toronto, I flew into Buffalo. I was going to rent a car, but this guy lived in the area and said I could ride in with him up to the meeting in Toronto. I came out of the airport, and he saw me and hollered for me to come over. When I got to his truck, it was one of those little deals, barely big enough to fit one grown man. But there we were, both having to cram in. He was 6'5 and I was 6'1, and on top of that, he had all kinds of junk stuffed in there. It was cramped, but at least we made it to our destination in two hours. It was one hell of an uncomfortable ride, but it was free.

We got there, went to our meeting, and then it was time to head home. That's when he decided to tell me he wasn't going back that way. I had to hail a taxi to the airport, but the flights were too rich for my blood. I didn't know how the hell I was going to get back, and was pretty aggravated with the man I had ridden in with. I couldn't say anything, though, he made me too much money. So I figured out I could take a bus. The bus took me a few miles down the road, and then the other passengers and I unloaded into a station wagon. By this time, it was snowing like crazy, and I was anxious to get to where I was going. But about midnight, the driver stopped and said he had to show me a place in Toronto. When we got there, it was a five-acre courtyard covered in five feet of snow. The lights were shining all over it, and it was a sight to see. Dazzling. I was happy to take in that view. Perhaps it was better that I didn't have to ride in the cramped little truck. As it turned out, I was able to catch a flight to Washington, D.C. that night and got home a little early.

MY THIRD MARRIAGE: 1999

Annette and I had been steadily dating since we met in 1995. I asked her to marry me, but we were both so busy with our careers that there wasn't much time for a wedding.

Annette jokes that she needed to test me before we married anyway. Her test was that if we could build a house together, we could have a successful marriage.

I had seen a house in a 1993 Southern Living magazine that I really liked, and we were able to agree on those plans. I hired an architect and a builder, but the architect had to draw the plans up several times before he finally got the front of the house facing the right direction. I didn't care about having any guest rooms, but Annette said our children might like to visit, so we added those.

As construction of our house was underway, and we hadn't killed each other yet, we decided it was time to plan for our wedding. The probate office must have thought we were crazy because we had to buy our marriage license three times before we ever found the time to tie the knot.

We finally set the date for January. It was the third marriage for both of us, and we promised that, come hell or high water, it would be the last. We asked my friend Dr. John David Hall, an Episcopal minister, to officiate the wedding, and he agreed. Since we had both been married before, we only wanted a simple ceremony at our new home.

Annette's guest list consisted of Faye, and my list was my three best friends— my dogs, Red, Lady, and Cassie. Red was a no-show, but we carried on with the ceremony despite his absence.

Even though our house wasn't completely finished, we decided to spend our wedding night there. There wasn't much time for a real honeymoon due to work, but we would have the rest of our lives for travel. Shocker, there was no hot water in the house. It was the quickest shower I ever took.

Annette and I kept our promise that this would be our last marriage, and like any marriage, it has had its ups and downs. We are alike in that we are both able to go our own ways in the morning when we go out the door, and we have been happy with that.

I guess I had my faults in my other marriages, and maybe in this one, too, at times. I can honestly say that I have been true blue to Annette. We are older now, and we continue to help and support each other.

Faye with me and Annette on our wedding day.

Red

Annette and I on our wedding day.

Lady

Cassie

Our wedding guest list included our three pets, Red, Lady and Cassie. Red was absent, but Lady and Cassie enjoyed the day.

DAD PASSES AWAY: 2003

At the end of May, we took Dad to the doctor, and they decided he needed to be admitted to the hospital. I didn't know it at the time, but he'd never make it back to what was left of his farm at Sauty Bottom.

Since Mom passed away, he had stayed pretty healthy. He didn't do any real farming anymore, but he kept busy. He had a big garden and every summer when everything started coming in, all the widows around would come by and he would load them up with corn and tomatoes and whatever else he had that needed picking.

He loved going to the senior center in Scottsboro to be with people his age. He even got himself a girlfriend, Fannie Pearl. But she died of cancer like Mom had.

When I wasn't traveling, I always stopped to check in on him before I headed home in the evenings, and on Sundays, he'd come by the house for supper.

In a lot of ways, Dad and I were the same person. We weren't the hold hands type. We kept our distance. I didn't tell him much, and he didn't ask much.

I'll never forget the moment I decided I would never come home and be a farmer like him. I still remember the two of us standing in the field. "Hey, Dad, why don't we rotate the crops over there this year?" That look on his face when he asked me, "What the hell do you know?"

Dad resting by one of his gardens.

Dad liked to be the boss. I think years down the road, I learned that I liked to be the boss too. When it comes to bosses, a farm is only big enough for one of them. Maybe that's why I took a different path.

Over the years, I'd tell Dad about my company, and sometimes I thought that he thought I was crazy. He never told me outright, but I think he was proud of my success even if I didn't follow in his footsteps exactly. I might have left the tractors behind, but we were both businessmen. Both entrepreneurs. Both the boss. Yes, I'm sure he was proud of me.

After the doctor admitted him to the hospital in Huntsville, Annette and I would stop by to visit him every day after work. Then one day, after he had been there about two weeks, they called to tell me that I had better get there fast. They didn't think he was going to make it long. His organs had started shutting down.

By the time I got there, he was gone.

He died on Thursday, June 12, and we buried him next to Mom the following Saturday.

Dad was 94. I don't guess anyone could say that his death was a surprise, but life was sure different without him around.

EXPANDING THE BUSINESS AGAIN: 2005

Business had been going okay, but it wasn't growing like I wanted. That's the thing with being an entrepreneur sometimes. It never feels like enough. You're always chasing the next big thing. In addition, I began to realize that competition in the market and added regulations to the industry were hampering the growth of ACSC.

We needed to add on to the business so that we would be legal in all of the states. That meant we either had to go through an outside insurance agency or create our own. I decided to create my own, and in the meantime, used an insurance company out of Nebraska.

I found an attorney to help me set up my insurance business, which we called Vehicle Services Insurance Company Risk Retention Group. The attorney helping me was an old man from Norman, Oklahoma. We traveled all over, setting up the company. It was not easy, but we got it done in under 15 months.

When all was said and done, my company could sell service contracts in as many as 40 states. Florida, in particular, had more requirements than some other states, so we had to start an entirely different business to sell our warranties there. We called it ACSC of Florida, and it was very lucrative in sales.

In 2005, along came a businessman from Oklahoma. He was a pitchman for a company selling auto warranties that needed a service company to accept and pay claims on the policies, which were sold by telemarketers. I could tell right away he was a conman. Still, I was intrigued by the idea.

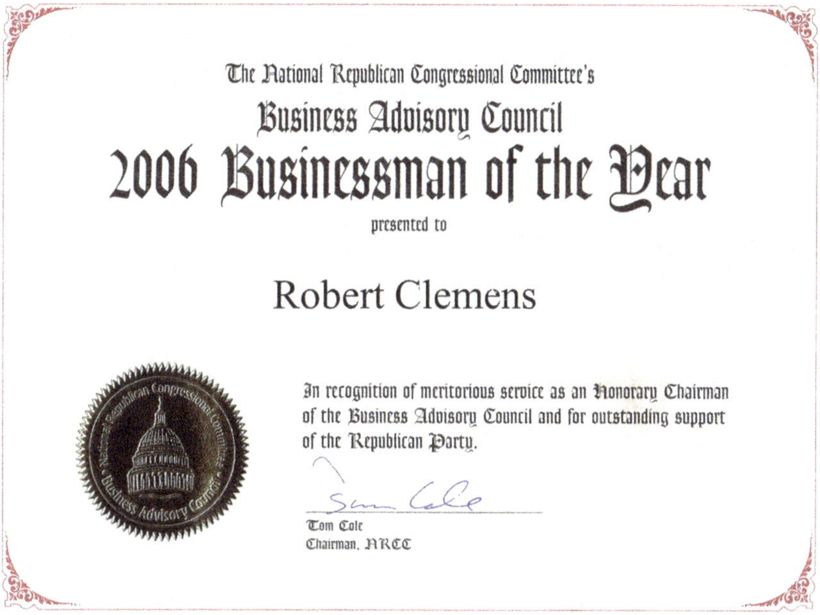

The National Republican Congressional Committee's

Business Advisory Council

2006 Businessman of the Year

presented to

Robert Clemens

National Republican Congressional Committee • Business Advisory Council

In recognition of meritorious service as an Honorary Chairman of the Business Advisory Council and for outstanding support of the Republican Party.

Tom Cole
Chairman, NRCC

In 2006, I was named businessman of the year by the National Republican Congressional Committee's business advisory council.

Besides, I always figured as long as I knew who I was dealing with, I could control him.

I'd been in the auto warranty business for years, but with this expansion, things got a bit more complicated. Now, instead of relying on salesmen and magazine ads, telemarketers would do our bidding. This added so many sales that I had to hire a team of people to make sure all of our bases were covered. Business grew so quickly that I needed a CEO, an IT professional, an accountant, and a claims officer. We called our new service Gold Key Protection.

Since our business began to rely on telemarketers, I decided I needed to see a telemarketing operation firsthand. My first visit to a telemarketing group was in St. Louis, Missouri. It was located inside a large warehouse. There were telemarketing personnel seated at about fifty desks across the warehouse. We had paid a marketing company to send mailers to people who had vehicles that were eligible for our mechanical warranty, and the workers were answering phone calls from the people who had received the postcard and were interested in learning more about the warranty.

During this time, we used around three different finance companies, and that usually worked out fine. When customers chose to pay the full amount up front with the telemarketers, it became a concern. The telemarketing companies sometimes failed to pay us, so when a customer filed a claim, there was no record that they had a warranty.

After dealing with this for a few years, I decided to start my own call center in Huntsville. I still owned a medium-sized building in another part of the city, and it had a vacancy. My top assistant wanted to supervise it, and we started by buying names, addresses, and phone numbers from marketing lists.

We bought a used call center system and installed it in the building. After a while, we didn't sell enough warranties this way to continue this part of the business. We decided to close up shop and move out. The call system was so out of date that we junked it. I sold the building and removed one of my headaches.

GOOD HELP IS HARD TO FIND: 2011

A decade into the new millennium, business was still booming, but it seemed that profits were not growing.

One day, a trusted member of my office staff asked me to meet her in the parking lot of a service station. There, away from the office, she let me know that my employees were flying first class all over the country, renting limos and eating fancy dinners on the company's dime. As someone who drives to Nashville before every flight because I know that's the cheapest way to fly, I was not too happy to learn that my staff was being so extravagant. Especially, since I personally still lodge at the damn BOQ or Days Inn.

The next day, I went to the office and pulled some of the invoices. Sure enough, the aforementioned was true. In addition, the invoices indicated that large sums of money were paid to marketers who falsified sales, and extra bonuses were being paid to the marketers for a sales volume that was false.

The next day, I dismissed the CEO and the IT person. I hired a forensic accountant, and the investigation revealed everything to be true.

We sued the parties involved, but by the time we went through the system, they had cleaned everything out. We got nothing and still had to pay our legal fees.

If I learned one lesson in all my years being a business owner, it's that in a lawsuit, the law firms are the only winners.

END OF AN ERA

Untrustworthy employees and customers who made false claims were enough to eventually sour me on the warranty business. Though it had made me a lot of money over the years, I finally decided to stop selling warranties.

The warranty business is one you can't simply walk away from, so for years we were there for our customers and honored the service contracts that we had sold. I let employees go and downsized as the warranties expired.

The last contract expired in December of 2019, and we began to focus solely on our import business. At one time, I'd had nearly forty employees, but in the end, all that was left was myself and my secretary, Sonya. She had always been knowledgeable about everything, and she was trustworthy. So, I kept her by my side.

In 2021, we shut down the Huntsville office and moved to Scottsboro, where we operated out of a closed-down Regions Bank building for a few years.

Since ending the warranty business, ACSC has continued to handle quite a few imports for the USDOT. As I entered my 90s, I decided it was time to think about closing the office. We have a few customers who import vehicles to the US that have been with us for many years, and we will continue to certify their imports. Other than that, the business has come to an end.

When I stopped selling warranties, there was a great deal of money in the bank, and it all belonged to me. Maybe that was the point. I decided

I didn't have to try so hard to be a success anymore. The millionaire status proved I already was one.

I guess you could say I am officially retired now.

The office gave me somewhere to go every day, but it wasn't work. Not like all those busy years I spent traveling the world and building my business.

My head tells me it is over, but it's hard to turn off the faucet.

THE LAST CHAPTER

I'm 91 now. I have a long life to reflect upon, and I thought writing a memoir was as good a way to do it as any. I think it's a pretty long and successful story. Maybe not some of the marriages, but everything else.

I was born and raised in a small town. Now I'm back there, living out my days barely a mile down the road from where my mama delivered me in 1933. In between here and there, I've had some wild rides. Through it all, I experienced ups and downs, chased a lot of women, and became a millionaire. Like anyone else, I made mistakes along the way. But it has been a good life, one I'm proud of.

A lot of people who start out like I did never make it too far from home. Their star burns out after high school. They get a job at the local mill, have a few kids, and that's that. I guess it was the Clemens' blood in me that made me want more. I couldn't have settled for topping out in high school. I wanted to do a lot with my life, and I wanted to be the best at all of it. The drive was something I was born with, but if someone were to ask me what the secret to a successful life is, I'd tell them you have to work at it. Nothing happens just because you want it to.

When you stay on this side of the dirt as long as I have, you find that you outlive a lot of people. Lil passed away in 2015 after a battle with Alzheimer's. We divorced a lifetime ago, but she was the mother of my three children and an important part of my story. Our daughter, Sue, passed away a few years later in 2018. I'll never forget when she was a baby and the doctor told us she would not live a very long life, but they were wrong. She lived to be 63, and I like to think that despite her disabilities, she lived a fulfilling life. My other girls, Sharon and Dawn, have carried on my bloodline and built families and lives of their own.

Dad passed away when he was 94. Lord knows I'm not going to let the old man outdo me on this one, so I figure I've got a few more years left yet to hang around. My health is not as good as I would like it to be, but I shouldn't complain. I still live at home, and I still drive a GMC truck with a 6.9-liter engine that many young men would kill to have. It would pull a damn freight train if I needed it to.

Some days I think I'd like to do more traveling, maybe take in another Green Bay Packers game at Lambeau Field. But other days, I'm content to stay in the comfort of the home that Annette and I built together. I enjoy the company of my cat. No one tells me what I can or can't do, and I never have to worry about money.

When the days are long, the memories of times gone by play like a motion picture in my head.

I close my eyes and take myself back to the glory days. I see myself on a football field that no longer exists. I'm a high school star. I've got a fan club. There are young girls who want to be my date to the banquet, and old men who like to see me tackle. The girls cheer from the bleachers, and the old men lean over the fence for a closer look. I hear the principal holler at them over the speaker as he calls the game, "Clemens off tackle for five yards. Get off that fence over there!" They don't pay him any mind. They are there to see me. They call me Bigfoot. Everything about me is big. And I am going to do great things.

CLEMENS' FARM
1848 - 2024

THE WALLY'S BOYS ASSOCIATION
HIGH FIVE RECOGNITION

ROBERT "FOOTS" CLEMENS

WE ARE PLEASED TO RECOGNIZE THIS HARDNOSED FULLBACK WHO DISTINGUISHED HIMSELF AT GEORGIA AND
ALSO WITH THE GREEN BAY PACKERS. A MAN WHO HAS EMBRACED LONGEVITY WHO "LUCKILY STILL DRIVES,
GOES TO HIS OFFICE, AND AS NEEDED, MANAGES HIS HUNTING CLUB (1500 ACRES) AND TRAVELS ALL OVER THE
SOUTH WEST TO TEXAS AND NORTH TO GREEN BAY," A DAMN GOOD DAWG AND GREAT AMERICAN.

APRIL 17, 2021
DATE
KIRBY SMART, HEAD FOOTBALL COACH

JOHN PAUL HOLMES, PRESIDENT

Scottsboro
AUTO AUCTION INC.

ABOUT THE AUTHOR

Robert "Bob" Norwood Clemens was raised near Scottsboro, Alabama, in a community called Sauty Bottom by the locals, where he was born in 1933.

Clemens is a graduate of Scottsboro High School, The University of Georgia and Golden Gate University. Clemens, known as "Big Foot" to his fans in Scottsboro, was a star football player in high school and was inducted into the first class of the Jackson County Sports Hall of Fame in 2014. While attending the University of Georgia, Clemens was a star fullback for the Bulldogs, where he was called "Foots." In Georgia, he earned an Academic All-SEC Choice Award in 1954, and in 2021 he was honored with a High Five Recognition by The Wally's Boys Association. His stellar performance on the football field led to an offer from the Green Bay Packers, where he played for one season before beginning his commitment to the United States Air Force in 1956.

During his 20 years of military service, Clemens served as a pilot on refueling aircrafts, flying both the KC-97 and KC-135 for missions supporting the Cold War and the Vietnam War. Clemens earned three Air Medals and a commendation medal over the course of his career. Upon his retirement, Clemens was awarded the Distinguished Flying Cross for extraordinary bravery in the Vietnam War.

When Clemens retired from the military, he set his sights on becoming a businessman. After a few ventures that didn't suit him, he became a pioneer in the vehicle extended warranty business and later he led the market for imported vehicle registration. Success with his company, Automobile Consumer Services Corporation, earned him several recognitions and awards over the years, including The National Republican Congressional Committee's Business Advisory Council 2006 Businessman of the Year Award.

Clemens served on numerous boards and civic organizations throughout the years, including Rotary International, Jackson County Republican Party, Alabama State Republican Committee and Retired Military Officers Association.

Clemens currently resides in Sauty Bottom, a few miles down the road from his birthplace, with his wife, Annette. He officially retired in 2024 at the age of 91.